SKILLS
THAT
BUILD

SKILLS THAT BUILD

The Hard Science of
Soft Skills for Work and Life

GINA M. WILSON, MS

Bayfront
Press

HOCKESSIN, DELAWARE, USA
2021

Published in the United States by Bayfront Press, and imprint of System Strategies, Hockessin Delaware, in 2021.

Cover and interior design by David Ter-Avanesyan/Ter33Design

Library of Congress Control Number: 2021909546

ISBN 978-1-7370829-0-3 (pb)

www.ginamwilson.com

Printed in the United States of America

For Zoe

CONTENTS

Acknowledgments   ix

Introduction   1

PART ONE: *The Art and Science of Connected Communications*

Chapter 1: Becoming Aware   7

Chapter 2: Effective Communication Matters   13

Chapter 3: Communication is Like Golf   31

Chapter 4: Upping Your Communications Game   46

Chapter 5: Lion or Lamb: The Communications Continuum   59

PART TWO: *You Don't Say: Empathic Listening and*
                   Nonverbal Communication

Chapter 6: It Takes Energy to Engage with Empathy   81

Chapter 7: Is Your Body Working For You or Against You?   95

Chapter 8: The Brain as Listening Organ   105

PART THREE: *Busy is the New Black: Fashionably Manage Your Time*

Chapter 9: There's No Time Like the Present   118

Chapter 10: In a Time Warp: The Perception of Time   139

Chapter 11: Cellphone, Smartwatch, Alexa: There's an App for That!
                                                                        162

PART FOUR: *Resilience: Learning to Thrive*

Chapter 12: Moving the Dial Toward Thriving   185

Chapter 13: Flowing Down the River of Human Performance 199

Chapter 14: Tipping the Positivity Scale   219

Afterword   241

Notes   242

About the Author   245

ACKNOWLEDGMENTS

I owe a great deal to the many researchers whose fascinating work initially inspired my love for the science of psychology, especially Elizabeth Loftus, Daniel Kahneman, and Martin Seligman. They posed questions and sought answers that stimulated my intellectual curiosity and consumed my mind for many years. Professors in my undergraduate days at the University of Delaware sparked in me such interest in psychology that I abandoned studying electrical engineering midway through. I am grateful to the psychology faculty at Villanova University who taught me the importance of empirical study and peer review in advancing the field as a scientific discipline. I also thank Barbara Fredrickson, Richard Ryan, and Mihaly Csikszentmihalyi, who rekindled my interest through their work in well-being, positive emotion, motivation, and optimal human performance. Their contributions in defining quantifiable behaviors have provided a valuable application of science to the coaching profession. I wish to thank the Institute of Coaching for its role in providing learning opportunities that advance the field of coaching through science.

This book would not have been possible without the insights gained from my clients, many of whom have taught me far more than they know. I thank them for trusting me as a partner on their journey and sharing their stories, challenges, and joys. Many thanks go out to those who read early versions of the book and provided invaluable feedback: Karen Redfearn, Carl Gartner, and especially Diane DeSantis Hoffman. Their contributions made this work immeasurably better. Thank you to Richard D. Templeton, Kelli Wilke. Special thanks go to David Ter-Avanesyan and Bridget Carrick, whose expertise and professionalism brought this book to fruition.

I am ever grateful to my husband, Kevin, for enduring endless discussions, acting as a springboard for ideas, providing honest critique and perspective, creating graphics, and most importantly, believing in this project. I thank my children, Christopher and Monica, for reading early versions with a critical eye and offering a millennial perspective. You continue to inspire.

Finally, I thank my parents, Helen and Frank DeSantis, who have instilled in me the value of education, hard work, respect for others, and kindness. Their love for their work as I was growing up gave me a true appreciation for how it contributes to a sense of self and life satisfaction. Their love for me inspires me to continually strive to be the best person I can be.

INTRODUCTION

Terence had been working for four years as an accountant in a small CPA firm. He had progressed enough in his job to be able to work independently and mentor junior accountants who came on board. His boss often complimented him on a job well done. However, when it came time for his latest performance review, Terence was disappointed to receive only a modest cost-of-living increase in pay despite the boss's accolades for quality work. He left the review feeling confused, concerned that his hard work was not being adequately recognized. The next day, Terence requested a meeting with his boss. This time, having prepared his thoughts and reviewing his accomplishments, Terence opened the meeting with an honest statement that reflected his concerns. "I am disappointed with the salary increase you presented at my performance review. I would like you to consider increasing my salary to reflect the quality of my work and my contributions to the firm." He proceeded to articulate his various successful projects, the training he had done for new hires, and the high level of client satisfaction he had earned. He emphasized the value he added to the company. In presenting his thoughts clearly, factually, and in a positive manner, Terence advocated for and allowed himself to be heard without disparaging his boss. He stated his request, provided facts, and left the door open for the boss to respond favorably.

Some might say that took guts, but guts had nothing to do with it. Terence was communicating assertively, which allowed him to preserve his self-respect while also respecting the boss. Terence had demonstrated the basic and powerful skill of assertive communications, a skill he had learned and continues to practice in situations at work and home.

We are forever seeking to understand our behavior and that of others, in both personal relationships and in the workplace. We find these behaviors are often not too different across settings. Efficacy in one area of life spills over to others. Someone having a difficult time at work finds that it affects their home life, and vice versa. We are whole beings, not compartmentalized as parent, student, boss, colleague, or friend. Our behaviors are simple and yet complex and often learned, and, as I show in this book, they can be changed for the better through awareness, motivation, training, and practice. Our behaviors influence how we think, how we act, and who we are, yet they are not fixed. They can be changed for the better. Many behaviors influence our well-being, and conversely, our well-being affects our behavior.

Certain behaviors impact our ability to succeed in the workplace. Communication, empathy, values-based prioritization, and resilience are four areas in which crucial behaviors, or the so-called soft skills, must be learned. We are not born with these complete and innate abilities, and our brains are programmed with biases and instincts that in some ways hinder more advantageous behaviors. But humans are born with a capacity to learn, persevere, and evolve as human beings in a social world. We have agency.

A lot has been written about success and what it takes. Books about success abound in any online or brick-and-mortar bookstore.

Often these writings stem from the perspective of a business guru or industry expert. They cite tangible skills associated with technical degrees, business acumen, or training. Leadership experts extol various virtues required for leading others and hawk new mindsets and trending practices. However, some skills, the soft skills, must first be learned and then evolve within those future leaders. Terence, although an accomplished accounting professional, benefited from having learned and continually improving communication behaviors that further enable him to succeed. The success in communicating well with his boss carries with him outside of his work too. It is satisfying. It feels good. It *builds*.

The absence of critical soft skills precludes the most able employee or supervisor from progressing in their career and moving into elusive leadership roles. Soft skills cut across all fields and occupations and form a solid foundation for success not only in one's career but also in life. In fact, people who practice these skills regularly report more satisfaction, less stress, and an improved outlook for their life and work. Schools typically do not teach these skills directly, as curriculums focus on more tangible hard skills. Emphasis on STEM (science, technology, engineering, and math) and extracurriculars leaves little room in students' busy schedules for learning and developing soft skills. Similarly, in the workplace, management devotes too little effort to professional development in the broader skills that benefit individuals yet ultimately also benefit the organization. In more than twenty-five years of consulting and coaching, whether the client is a C-suite executive, midcareer professional, college student, or recent college graduate, I've found that poor interpersonal communications, lack of empathy, absence of self-care and wellness practices, inability to bounce back after setbacks, and poorly focused time are common roadblocks. They can derail even the most intelligent, highly credentialed, accomplished adult.

Roundtables of business owners and corporate executives alike lament the inadequate professionalism, consumer focus, and basic skills among new hires that could better position these employees for success in the work environment. Yet these skills can be learned and mastered. Soft skills taught in adolescence can buffer against the inevitable hardships of teenage years and better prepare students for challenges faced in college and adulthood. Even the most seasoned professionals can further improve their skills by learning new practices emerging from the latest research. It is never too early or too late to grow. Millennials, Gen Xers, and baby boomers alike can benefit from trying out new techniques and honing existing skills. Learning these techniques and behaviors benefits the individual by establishing a solid base on which other-focused leadership skills and wellness practices can build. Without them, the leadership house of cards will fall. The individual who first builds the self has set the virtual concrete in place on which to construct a solid house of life.

A growing body of science shows what happens in the body and brain when using these skills effectively. There is compelling evidence that by incorporating these behaviors regularly into our repertoire, we experience lasting physiological and psychological health benefits. These behaviors are good for body, brain, business, and the bottom line.

This book not only presents the case for why soft skills are important but also shares scientific findings and techniques for readers to coach themselves. It offers stories of how these practices have been applied by coaching clients to realize results they set out to achieve. Exercises included throughout the chapters will give you, the reader, a chance to apply techniques grounded in science, to improve your own skills and ultimately reap both physical and mental health benefits. I invite you to become empowered with these skills that build from within. In developing the four skill sets—communication, empathy, values-based prioritization, and resilience—you will add crucial assets to your success tool kit and can begin to build the reserves that will buffer you against inevitable challenges and setbacks in work and life.

PART ONE
THE ART AND SCIENCE OF CONNECTED COMMUNICATIONS

CHAPTER 1
Becoming Aware

Communication between people sounds so simple. After all, babies learn to talk in the first years of life. But as we all know, talking is not the same as communicating. Verbal communication and spoken dialogue between people involve a complex interaction of instinctive and learned skills, many of our physical senses, and even our bodies. No matter how much training we've had, we can all become better communicators. Our skills can be honed to improve as communicators in the workplace—with colleagues, bosses, employees, students, and clients—and also in our personal communications with family and friends and in the community. Perhaps more importantly, learning to better communicate has lasting implications for our overall health and well-being. In this chapter, we begin to explore the best practices for effective communications through observing helpful behaviors that enhance communications and bad habits that interfere with understanding.

Communication, Good and Bad

Most people are familiar with the old Abbott and Costello comedy routine "Who's on First," in which they discuss players on a baseball team.[1] An excerpt of the transcript is shown below.[2] This hilarious sketch is well known for its portrayal of communication of words that make sense, yet the participants clearly do not understand each other. It is a great example of communications gone wild. While wildly funny, there is so much we can learn from it about communications.

> *Costello: I'm asking you who's on first.*
>
> *Abbott: That's the man's name.*
>
> *Costello: That's who's name?*
>
> *Abbott: Yes.*
>
> *Costello: Well go ahead and tell me.*
>
> *Abbott: That's it.*
>
> *Costello: That's who?*
>
> *Abbott: Yes.*

Aside from making us laugh, while watching the video of this sketch and really focusing in on the mechanics of their communication, it becomes clear that Abbott and Costello demonstrate some effective communication behaviors.

What went well?

✓ They were completely absorbed in each other.

✓ They made eye contact with each other.

✓ Each often repeated what the other had said— repetition for clarification.

✓ Each often restated the question.

✓ They used their hands and bodies for emphasis.

So, what went wrong? Clearly also an example of poor communication on so many levels, several maladaptive behaviors derailed this exchange:

✗ Body language cues did not help convey the message. There were undesirable behaviors by both parties: crossed arms, throwing their hands up, pointing fingers, looking away, stamping feet, rolling eyes, using the "stop" hand, and shaking the head.

✗ They raised their voices, often shouting at each other.

✗ Each frequently interrupted the other.

✗ They were so quick to answer, never pausing to consider what was being said.

✗ Assumptions prevented them from discerning the other's meaning. Preconceived notions of names impeded their understanding and reduced comprehension of possibilities.

✗ Perhaps one of the most glaring omissions in this communication, however, was the lack of questioning to clarify what was meant.

And while many of us laugh at this absurd sketch, we inadvertently exhibit some of these same behaviors in our own communications. It is easy to watch a skit and point out flaws. However, only when we become aware of our own habits, behaviors, and pitfalls can we work to change or refine them and ultimately improve ourselves.

In coaching, we work from the perspective that clients are their own best coach. That is, we believe that clients know what solutions are best for them and how they can best overcome challenges. It is the coach's job to draw that out and help the client articulate solutions, goals, and means for achievement. But this requires a great deal of self-awareness and supportive efforts. Coaches provide that level of support, encourage self-awareness and accountability, and facilitate reflection so real accountability and progress toward change can be made. Even without a coach, we can all tune in and become more aware of what's going on within a communication. We can start by observing ourselves (and others) for dysfunctional behavior patterns that we can learn to avoid, then replace undesirable behaviors with more effective and positive alternatives. Awareness of communication styles is the first step in becoming a better communicator.

Communications Awareness Exercise

1. Becoming aware of communication behaviors is necessary in order to distinguish between those that enhance and detract from understanding. By first observing others, then ourselves, we can begin to understand their influence. This exercise will help you identify and then focus on improving specific behaviors you commonly exhibit.

2. Look for opportunities to be an active observer of a serious conversation between two real people (not on a television show or in a movie). It can be an overheard conversation in a restaurant, on the train, or at the coffee station at work. Most public places offer opportunities to observe people talking with others. Try to observe and note some of the behaviors the speakers and listeners exhibit—both positive and negative ones that impact the conversation.

3. It is easier to observe others than ourselves. Unless you have a webcam in your home or office, most of us have little opportunity to see ourselves communicating in live action. Think about a recent conversation you've had with someone important in your life—a family member, friend, colleague, or boss. Reflect on what went well (for example, undivided attention, eye contact, repeating for clarification, restating questions, etc.) and what went wrong (for example, closed body language, interrupting, formulating a response while the other person is talking, assumptions, etc.). Write these thoughts down. Circle the behaviors that you exhibited—both good and bad. Are these common characteristics of your general communications, or were they specific to that situation? Why?

4. From that list of observed behaviors, make another list of any that hindered good communication on a three-by-five-inch index card or sticky notes. For each behavior on your card, write the positive alternative in bold or all-capital letters next to it to remind yourself what you are trying to do. For example, if interrupting is on your list, the alternative behavior you want to replace it with may be to take a deep breath and count to three. Post this in a prominent location where you will see it daily, such as on your bathroom mirror, the refrigerator, a virtual note on your computer screen, or your car's dashboard. Choose one behavior each week to focus on and make a conscious effort to eliminate that negative behavior and replace it with a more positive alternative. Focusing on only one specific behavior for a period of time gives you a chance to practice, incorporate changes gradually, and build

success on one skill at a time. (Trying too many new behaviors at once can backfire and become overwhelming enough to cause you to give up.) If the behavior persists after the week, try it for another week before moving on to another one. Generally, after three consecutive weeks, a behavior becomes more second nature and habits begin to form. You can work through your list this way until you've dedicated focused effort on each behavior you identified for improvement.

5. Once you've worked through your list, repeat step 2, and note the changes in your communication patterns. Notice how your list of negative patterns has diminished. Congratulate yourself on the awareness, hard work, and new skills you've developed!

CHAPTER 2
Effective Communication Matters

Behind our daily habits and experiences lies a fascinating science, and in applying these findings, we can learn many practical techniques to guide our communication behavior and begin to understand the changes these interactions can elicit in the brain. Maybe you've noticed that on days during which you haven't spoken to another person, you feel less satisfied, perhaps more irritable or less energetic. Or on days when it seems like nothing but bad news is coming your way, you find yourself less productive, less creative, or drowning in negative thoughts. These observations and more have been the subjects of rigorous study in labs and beyond to see just what is happening in the brain and body.

Communication Is a Basic Need

As a coach, I attend conferences, review research papers and scientific journals, and participate in industry training to continually develop my practice and learn from prominent scientists. Two influential contributors are Dr. Richard Ryan, an authority at the University of Rochester on adult development and intrinsic motivation, and Dr. Barbara Fredrickson, a social psychologist and positive emotion researcher at University of North Carolina.

In 2000, Ryan and his research partner, Edward Deci, formulated the self-determination theory of motivation. They described three basic psychological needs that impact psychological health and well-being: relatedness, autonomy, and competency.

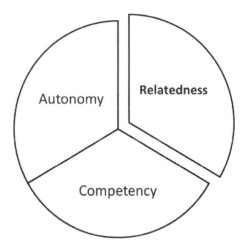

Figure 2.1: Three basic psychological needs

Like the familiar basic physical needs—food, water, shelter—Ryan and Deci found that the three psychological needs are also crucial to wellness and therefore should not be ignored.[3] Their studies show that failure to meet these needs not only inhibits psychological health but reduces our ability to function optimally within our environment as well. Their basic psychological needs theory (BPNT) argues that our psychological well-being and optimal functioning is contingent on three things: relatedness, autonomy, and competence. They defined *relatedness* as "desire to feel connected to others." It can be expressed through our communications. Situations that foster relatedness have been shown to positively impact wellness. Interacting with others is a means to satisfy this basic psychological need. (Competency and autonomy are discussed in later chapters.) Failure to meet the relatedness need contributes to suboptimal human functioning. We cannot underestimate the power of psychological needs; unmet, they become devastating physical manifestations. Our life goals, motivation, and personal happiness are enabled only after having met the three basic needs. Failure to meet these important psychological needs results in a lack of thriving.

Many workplaces have changed significantly since the onset of the COVID-19 pandemic. One major change for many businesses is the shift to working remotely. So new to many workplaces, remote work posed considerable challenges not only from a technical and logistical perspective but also in team connectivity. Teams had to adapt to the change.

Mandy, a managing director in a consulting firm, had enjoyed a highly productive team that worked on-site at various client locations and came together in the office weekly. During the pandemic, her team went to 100 percent remote work, no client on-site work and no weekly headquarter meetings. While initially popular among her consultants, this arrangement quickly deteriorated as individual consultants had fewer opportunities to interact with each other, pick the brains of their colleagues, and work alongside their clients. They used instant messaging online, and many turned off the camera during video calls. In short, the team had lost opportunities for relatedness. Mandy made a few changes to restore the connectivity of her team, and morale improved. She established a protocol whereby the first ten minutes of a weekly team call was dedicated to individuals sharing any non-work-related challenges, thoughts, and concerns they were experiencing during the pandemic restrictions and to celebrate any good news, small or large. The team was encouraged to replace instant messaging with actual phone calls to their coworkers and clients. Twice a month, the team decided to use the last hour of a workday to take turns conducting a fun, hands-on class for each other, including creative crafts, special recipes, and exotic cocktails. These efforts enabled the team to connect with each other in ways that promoted connection and created relatedness opportunities in the new normal workplace.

Our ability to effectively communicate contributes significantly to our ability to thrive and satisfies the important relatedness component of BPNT:

✓ a desire to feel connected to others

✓ universally rated as one of the most important values

✓ often neglected in the workplace, schools, clinical environments

✓ contributes to well-being and optimal human functioning

How have you connected today? By effectively communicating with others, we support the feelings of being connected and related, and therefore we improve our well-being and optimal functioning as people in communities and workplaces. Ryan and others studied the basic psychological needs and motivation in many different settings and populations: teachers and students; exercise enthusiasts; principal and teacher; parents; working adults; retirees; multicultural populations (Russian, German, Israeli, Korean, and Canadian); and across occupations including business, education, medicine, law, and sports.[4]

Interestingly, relatedness is universally rated as one of the most important values yet is often one of the most neglected aspects in the workplace, schools, and even clinical environments. Though the need for human relatedness and communication is innate, we now know that regular, effective communication is a vital, learned behavior that improves with practice and has a measurable impact on health and well-being. For the workplace, this is important because wellness and optimal functioning increase job satisfaction and buy-in—more so than status and pay! Communicating and connectedness at work not only improve an individual's well-being and performance, they ultimately benefit the organization itself. Let's look now at ways to improve relatedness opportunities in the workplace.

Motivation

Ryan and Deci's self-determination theory (SDT) also examines the impact and sources of motivation. They explain two types of motivation: intrinsic and extrinsic.

Intrinsic motivation is especially important in coaching because the client must articulate and establish goals for the process to be successful. These goals must be set *by* the client, not *for* the client. As a coach, I cannot set your goals. Your boss or friend cannot set your goals. Only you can do this, and by doing so, you are exercising motivation and will reap the rewards of your achievement toward those goals. If you experience enjoyment from progressing with those goals, it reinforces your motivation and energizes you to do more toward the desired state. And long after the coaching has finished, clients who experience intrinsic motivation are better able to sustain their efforts and goal-directed behaviors. SDT focuses on intrinsic motivation, that which comes from within, and its causes.

Extrinsic motivation is external to the self. You may be rewarded, but the source of reward is not the sheer joy of the behavior—it comes from another person or outside force. Expecting a reward or recognition and avoiding punishment (job loss or lack of promotion) are examples of extrinsic sources of motivation. Knowing you will get the boss's approval for giving a stellar presentation to customers may motivate you to improve your communication, but these boosts are more episodic and generally short-lived and unsustainable. Knowing you have mastered public speaking and have developed skills to comfortably present to a group without experiencing debilitating stage fright or ridicule is something you feel from within. Experiencing this intrinsic motivation is more likely to strengthen you with lasting behaviors that you internalize.

At work, it is easy to blame the boss, coworkers, or the company when things are not going well, especially when you are being passed up for opportunities you feel you deserve. Initiative for changing the situation could come from within (intrinsic motivation), such as when you determine you want to learn a new skill and you enjoy doing so. Or the initiative could be externally motivated; for example, if the boss informs you that you must go to a specific training (presumably to improve your value to the company). Knowing you must go to keep your job, you comply. While wanting to keep your job is motivating, the force behind it is only external and less likely to be enjoyable. If you set the goal and recognize the value of the acquired skill, you are more likely to follow through with the training and enjoy the experience. Being forced to take a training class is also not likely to produce the same feelings of satisfaction had you chosen the class for yourself.

Intrinsic motivation leads to results that are more likely to stick with you, improves your ability to achieve your goals, and fosters optimal performance more so than extrinsic motivation (see figure 2.2). In coaching sessions, sometimes a client initially finds motivation externally and exhibits goal-directed behaviors in an effort to please the coach or meet the accountability demands they had set. However, a skillful coach will work with the client to elicit perceived benefits of the behavior from the client's perspectives so they can internalize their own reasons for wanting to do it. This guides the motivation toward intrinsic sources and is much more successful in cultivating behavior change.

Figure 2.2: Sources of motivation

Intrinsic	Extrinsic
elicits internal rewards	elicits external rewards
desire/pleasure model	incentive/punitive model
generated within self	contingent on others

Once you decide on a behavior you want to change, a good practice is to identify what benefits you might realize once you start exercising that behavior. Imagine how life or work—or both—will be better once you are doing the desired behavior routinely. Visualize the joy you will experience as a result of the behavior, and you will be on your way to developing more lasting, sustainable intrinsic motivation.

Since connection with others is intrinsically satisfying, opportunities for coworkers to connect with each other result in increased satisfaction on the job. An important conclusion for the workplace, from Ryan and Deci's research, is that when an employer fosters a relatedness-supported environment at work, staff enjoy the benefits of intrinsic motivation for connectivity, which promotes their own optimal functioning. Cultivating communications among staff and supporting successful interactions between people allows them to develop intrinsic motivation. Fostering connectedness within the workplace will further enhance the well-being and performance of individuals and ultimately performance of the organization itself. Our psychological health, and the health of our workplace, matters.

How can we increase relatedness on the job? Rethinking how we work can open possibilities with little investment. Meetings can be held in-person occasionally to supplement conference calls. Teams can opt for video chat when appropriate. The physical environment can be modified by removing physical barriers between offices or establishing communal areas for people to gather informally. Often the lunchroom or coffee station becomes a connection point. Much more can be done. Management can create opportunities for employee engagement—inside the office and outside of work—to give employees a chance for informal camaraderie, to volunteer in the community together, or to exchange ideas or share common interests. Tall office partitions that impede sight lines among staff could be replaced with shorter partitions or eliminated. Small gathering areas or spaces to collaborate could be established in an unused office or storage room to promote interaction and collaboration. Whiteboards can be mounted in common spaces for idea sharing, goal setting, or messaging. Anything that can be done to reduce isolation and promote interaction among and across teams will help create opportunities for relatedness and thereby improve intrinsic motivation while cultivating well-being.

Some workplaces practice Agile techniques, in which team members gather daily for a brief "stand-up" meeting (where no one sits down to help quicken the process) to share progress on a project. Others use staff meetings, town hall gatherings, off-site challenge courses, or even concert events to connect. Anything an employer can do to facilitate interaction between employees will help people satisfy that important relatedness need and enable them to function more optimally at work through intrinsic motivation.

Language Can Change How We Think

Language has been shown to be a direct contributor to our thoughts and attitudes. Simply changing how you state an idea influences your thoughts and behaviors. By rephrasing something, we can change negative thoughts to more hopeful and positive ones that offer possibility and open our minds to alternative ways of thinking and behaving.

For example, consider someone trying to lose weight. They can easily think, "I'm not losing weight on this diet, so I may as well go back to the way I was eating in the first place." We can conclude from this statement (a) they are frustrated, (b) they have not lost weight, and (c) they want to give up. Reframing this with different language changes the tone of the statement and offers the possibility of hope, paving the way for more positive behavior and thinking: "While I haven't lost weight yet on this diet, I am working hard to stay on it and am learning to make better food choices, which ultimately will improve my health and eventually take off the pounds."

This subtle change in language still acknowledges that no weight has been lost yet but emphasizes the learning and positive behaviors being exercised and opens the possibility of future improvements to health and weight loss.

You can envision the scowl of the first statement turning to a more hopeful facial expression with the second. This example shows how changing the language of a statement can impart a more hopeful and positive attitude, reinforcing goal-directed behavior. We allow for the possibility that the pounds will come off and the fact that we are developing better eating habits. We acknowledge the disappointing reality that progress is less than we had hoped for but regard it as a temporary state. The words have us looking forward, aspiring for better, with a confirmation that success is underway. When we choose our words wisely, we can impact our own behavior and thoughts, moving them in a more positive, constructive direction.

Language and Authority

Help desk supervisor Aaron found himself suddenly with a rather inexperienced team of service representatives. Due to turnover, one medical leave, and team expansion, there were now four new representatives in a team of seven. The more-senior members were complaining of the time they had to spend helping the newer reps, which they saw as impacting their performance volumes. The newer reps expressed frustration at not wanting to interrupt the others but needing answers in order to proceed. Aaron initially composed a directive, which he presented to the team, informing all that he expected the senior staff to help train the junior staff and that they must learn to work together. He instructed them to spend no more than ten minutes in on-the-spot training so that the targeted call wait times could be met. Time-off requests would not be granted until the team became more cohesive and wait times were brought down to a reasonable metric. Aaron was certain his directive would solve the challenges both junior and senior representatives were facing.

Unfortunately, Aaron's response to the teams' concerns was not well received and generated more confusion and frustration, with no improvement in call wait times over a one-week period. Aaron arrived for his coaching session stressed and exacerbated. As a supervisor, he felt entitled to set the expectations and tell his team how to resolve the conflicts. We reviewed his instructions together and examined the words he used and how the ideas were communicated to his team. Aaron realized his language came across as if he were not really listening to their concerns. By setting the ten-minute time limit, he was not allowing the members to work out for themselves how best to resolve their training needs. He had not invited any ideas or opinions from the team but instead simply told them what to do.

Workplaces are typically imbued with a formal or informal top-down hierarchy, from owner or leader, manager, and supervisor to the most entry-level associates. There is always someone in a position of authority, a decision-maker who sets the rules and defines what work is to be done and how. Many theories exist on how authority figures impact the performance of subordinates, with a focus on how to structure and delegate work effectively. Ryan and Deci studied particularly how an authority figure's language influences the intrinsic motivation of a subordinate in studies over a period of fifteen years across a wide variety of situations—within families, in the lab, in groups of undergraduates, and directly in the workplace. They looked for factors that enable individuals to meet their psychological needs while in a lower-power position, observing employees with their boss, students with faculty, and children with parents. The research revealed that when authorities use controlling language or fail to take the subordinate's perspective into account, people in the lower-power positions fail to (1) find intrinsic motivation, (2) internalize values, and (3) derive well-being benefits from that interaction. Controlling language uses coercion and directives like *should* and *must* and does not offer a chance for opinions, ideas, or comments to be exchanged. In the workplace, controlling language often includes rigid deadlines, references to consequences, and words like *compliance, mandates,* and *directives.* It may also involve close supervision, micromanagement, and little flexibility in how a task is done.

Controlling language and insensitivity toward another person served to *de-motivate* the person in the lower-power position. This has enormous implications for interactions we might have at home, at work, and any time we are trying to influence another person's actions when we are in a perceived higher-power position. If, as a boss or parent, we use controlling language, the other person in the exchange is less likely to internalize the values we are trying to communicate, and their motivation to comply with requests we make significantly decreases. Controlling language works against us and is likely to produce the opposite of our desired result.

How do we use language to motivate and benefit others? We can create a relatedness-supportive environment. This takes conscious and deliberate effort to establish a culture of supportive communication. The following are characteristic behaviors of a supportive communicator:

- ✓ conveying respect for the other person

- ✓ enabling the other person to feel valued and significant

- ✓ offering care and concern when challenges are shared

These behaviors elicit buy-in; increase compliance, job satisfaction, and motivation; and, at work, can be more motivating than status and pay. By building environments in which we foster meaningful connections among people, everyone benefits.

In Aaron's coaching sessions, we discussed the ideas behind intrinsic motivation and authority-figure language. Considering this, Aaron decided to meet again with the team. This time, he structured his communication in such a way to allow his team to voice their concerns and ideas. He voiced his interest in helping them all move forward in a positive way. He first stated his understanding of the problem, then allowed each person on the team to express their perspective in their own words. Aaron asked for their ideas: many expressed concern with the ten-minute time frame, while others worried about the increased call wait times. Aaron acknowledged their concerns and ideas. He compiled notes and told the team he would consider their input and rethink how training would occur. He thanked them for participating and sharing their thoughts. This approach was received much better. The team felt they had been listened to and that their ideas were heard and validated; they also saw Aaron's sincerity in devising a workable solution. He avoided using language like *should, must,* and imperative statements with fixed time frames. He began asking and stopped telling. His language changed not only his behavior but also that of his team. It changed attitudes as well. Aaron felt more confident in his abilities, and the team felt more hopeful and satisfied with their work.

Positivity

Communication cannot happen in a vacuum. It is surrounded by and generates emotion whether intentionally or not. Psychologist Barbara Fredrickson studied communication and positive emotion. Fredrickson's research tells us that connection is an important source of positive emotion, which has critical implications for physical and mental health.[5] Her work on positivity demonstrates physical implications of experiencing positive emotion and quantifies just how much positivity in relation to negativity we must experience to sustain mental health and perform at our best. Much of the work in positive emotion uses modern imaging techniques, such as functional MRIs, to show changes within the brain during specific behaviors and activity. Physiological measurements, including imaging and blood tests, are obtained during real-world situations and problem-solving to detect changes in the brain and body.

The work of Fredrickson and others shows that experiencing positive emotion elicits significant physiological changes in heart rate (cardiac vagal tone), blood pressure, and levels of oxytocin, a naturally occurring hormone that strengthens human bonds. (During birth, oxytocin forges mother-infant bonding.) Positive emotion allows the brain to take in more information, promotes big-picture thinking, improves memory, inspires creativity, and enables us to consider more possibilities within a situation. It even improves our ability to manage stress. We become more aware. And the impact of positive emotion has lasting effects, especially if we experience mild and frequent instances of positive emotion, according to Fredrickson. The magnitude of positivity is less important than the frequency for lasting physiological effects.

Communicating with others is perhaps one of the easiest ways to elicit positive emotion. Positive interactions enable connections with others, and as we learn from Fredrickson, connecting with others increases our sense of well-being. Her broaden-and-build theory of positivity paints the picture of a swinging door of awareness in the brain: our minds open and close with the presence and absence of positivity. Positivity promotes more global thinking, a trait crucial to a thinking organization. Her research spans boardrooms, work groups, college campuses, and international communities and has replicated the findings across numerous situations to scientifically confirm the unequivocal impact of sincere positivity. Any way in which we can introduce more positivity into our everyday lives will improve our well-being. Unless we live in utter isolation, communication is one way to easily create more positive emotion. Both Ryan and Deci's self-determination theory and Fredrickson's positive emotion research call for positive communications as a means to this greater end. And Fredrickson's finding that mild and frequent experiences of positivity are enough to effect a change demonstrates the feasibility for normal people to benefit from the practice. There is no need for a win-the-lottery magnitude of positivity; she talks of small wins as a means for change. Frequent and mild experiences cumulatively combine to grow enough emotion that ultimately makes a lasting difference. She describes an upward spiral of positivity.

Positive communication empowers us through these common factors:

✓ creates a feeling of positivity

✓ enables connections with others

✓ increases our sense of well-being

✓ motivation exists along a continuum

✓ enjoyment itself motivates

✓ small wins prime the pump

✓ upward spirals of change

By means of connected, positive communications, adults can typically satisfy the needs for both self-expression and relatedness through their personal interactions with others. Simply put, we find conversing with others satisfying. It becomes an intrinsic motivator. It's okay to do an activity simply because we find it interesting and enjoyable. Science has shown that doing things that delight us physically improves our health. When we think of an upward spiral, most of us will unconsciously look up and may even feel our chin lifting. The emotion elevates us and builds on itself. We can all develop ways to foster that intrinsic motivation and build the positive, connected communications within our home and workplace. In doing so, we reap the benefits, as do those with whom we interact. We build trust, and others will want to communicate with us; we feel valued and connected. We improve our self-esteem and that of others. We experience a sense of well-being and competency. The bottom line is that connected and positive communications is a healthy behavior for us as people, within a community, family, and organization.

I once heard Benjamin Zander, the conductor of the Boston Philharmonic Orchestra, speak about his book *The Art of Possibility*.[6] Zander, an engaging speaker and animated septuagenarian, described his job in this way: "I am in the business of shining eyes!" According to Zander, if what he is doing as a conductor is not affecting people in such a way that elicits emotion and enjoyment, he is not doing his job. He measures his success on his ability to bring about positive experiences in others. He told a story of how he takes groups of young musicians on a world tour as a youth orchestra. At the beginning of the months of practice, he instructs his musicians to write a letter to themselves to be opened in nine months. He tells them to write about the person they want to be at the end of the tour, specifically to "imagine the possibilities!" This exercise helps them envision a better musician, a better—and perhaps more mature—self, and they can visualize what is possible after all the practices and by participating in the orchestra and tour. Nine months later, the students were surprised to realize how much the letter influenced their development over that time, even those who initially balked at the idea of writing a letter to themselves.

The power of imagining the future is crucial to developing motivation toward a goal. I employ this technique in my coaching practice with individuals and organizations. I ask clients to project what life or work could be like in the future once progress is made toward set goals by asking, "What will your life be like once you have made the leap to the new [career, school, relationship, etc.]? What changes do you see in yourself? How have your relationships changed as a result? What has changed about your day-to-day life?" Questions like these invite retrospection and reflection on the specific results we might hope to achieve. By looking ahead and envisioning ourselves in the new context or with the new behaviors and skills, we put some tangible outcomes within sight that will serve to motivate us toward that end. I invite you to become a better communicator. As Benjamin Zander might say, "Imagine the possibilities."

Communications Vision Exercise

If you want to commit to improving your communications skills over the next three to six months with techniques you will learn in this book, start by writing a letter of what you envision yourself to be at the end of that period. Within the framework of the self-determination theory and positive emotions, ask yourself these questions:

- What are your goals for your own communication?

- What would you hope to learn?

- How will you be different?

- What will your communications be like at that time?

Take a lesson from Benjamin Zander and imagine the possibilities! Write the letter to yourself, seal it, mark your calendar for six months from today, and put it away to be opened then.

CHAPTER 3
Communication Is Like Golf

What does it take to become a better communicator, and how do we do it? What techniques should we be using to communicate more effectively? Some specific behaviors and practices will improve our ability to connect and communicate with others. Anyone who has tried to learn something new, like how to golf or play the piano, can appreciate the basic techniques that must be acquired and refined before they can become proficient. The same is true of communications.

Communication Fundamentals

You might consider yourself a good golfer if you regularly score in the low seventies or have a low handicap. A pianist might set her sights on playing Chopin's E-flat Major Nocturne or Beethoven's Moonlight Sonata. Golfers and pianists have a clear idea of what proficiency might look like, but how can we define effective communication? What would be the milestones of progress or proficiency?

Let's start by identifying some of the components for effective communication:

✓ An exchange exists between speaker(s) and listener(s).

✓ All parties experience both roles during the exchange.

✓ Both speaker and listener feel it was successful.

✓ Both feel they have been heard and understood.

✓ Both feel validated.

The experience was positive or neutral (no one was left feeling worse than before the exchange).

It is so important for a communication to be considered as a two-way interaction or exchange. It is not a speech, lecture, or interrogation. Rather it is more like a give and take, a gently swinging pendulum of dialogue. All people involved participate and engage. Both sound and silence ensue, a pause and play, giving time to reflect as well as speak. There is no steady cadence, stopwatch, or pressure. Sadly, many people say they've never had the luxury of communicating in this style. I believe this is because many of us have never learned the skills for being good communicators. We have learned to talk, but can we express ourselves? We have learned to keep quiet, but are we listening? We may have even learned patience, but are we really present?

Becoming a better communicator is a lot like learning to golf. You can master definite skills. You might read how to do it, take lessons from a professional, or play every Sunday to develop and keep up your skills. It takes practice and consistent play to master. Few, if any, perfect the practice. You may experience setbacks, develop bad habits, and feel plenty of frustration. Then you achieve shining moments. Golfers experience more enjoyment as time goes on and their abilities improve. Just as an aspiring pianist must learn basic components to read music, play scales, express dynamics, count out rhythms, and learn fingering, aspiring communicators must learn some basic components. Consider the following behaviors for effective communications:

- ✓ stay in the moment

- ✓ be aware

- ✓ unlearn bad habits

- ✓ acquire new skills

- ✓ show empathy

- ✓ use language effectively

- ✓ practice

Traditionally, personality researchers categorized people in certain ways based on their traits, such as introvert, extrovert, passive, aggressive, emotional, or task oriented. While these classifications might be useful at times, current research in personality suggests we all exhibit some of these traits at different times and our traits move along a continuum depending on situational circumstances. For effective communication, we have no single fixed trait to wield. We strive to understand where we are "in the moment" and what situational factors are influencing us at that very time. Perhaps more important is the ability to understand where the other person is at that moment in the shared conversation

In the moment refers to the idea of the here and now. Many people bring baggage and preconceived notions with them to a communication encounter. For instance, when starting to talk to Derek, you might start recalling the last time you spoke with him and make presumptions based on that conversation. If you hear "Let's talk," you might consider it a forewarning of an impending unpleasant exchange. Instead, I encourage you to let go of that baggage, start fresh, and take that very moment as a new opportunity. You may be entering into a conversation with a harried state of mind, having just sat in a traffic jam or received disturbing news just moments before. Or you may be distracted with a more pressing issue going on at home—the school nurse just called, and your child is sick. Any situational factor can influence your ability to be fully present in communicating with others. Much of the practice of mindfulness depends on such awareness and acknowledgment of where we are in the moment. And, even if you are in the moment of the conversation at hand, it is very possible that your communicating partner is not.

Being aware of where you *and* the other person are in the moment sets the stage for your interaction. Maybe the other person just received bad news, just sat in traffic, or is preoccupied with a mile-long to-do list. We frequently have no idea what we are carrying along to our conversations. It takes conscious effort to look deep inside yourself and acknowledge your own present. The next step, then, is to begin considering the other person's present. You may be ready for an exchange, but they may not be. Being sensitive to what others might have going on at the time of your conversation is critical to understanding how outside influences impact communication.

For effective communication, it is important to be aware of our own styles and patterns of communicating, and then we can begin to understand the patterns of communication in others. I use the analogy of the years of ingrained repetition of a bad golf swing: it is so hard to undo it! Just as the golfer must unlearn some old habits—change her grip, drop the left shoulder, relax the back, align the feet, and learn new ways to ultimately improve the swing—we must also unlearn old maladaptive speaking habits and make changes to become better communicators. Often, we know what we are doing wrong, but sometimes it takes an outside observer to help identify pitfalls. As a coach I often shadow clients in situations where they are struggling and then provide them with feedback and observations. With this information they can examine their behaviors more closely and determine what they want to change. Even without a coach shadowing you, you can reflect on your own behaviors and solicit feedback from others to gain a better understanding of what you are doing right and what needs work.

Golfers might envision how the ball will fall on a grade or put in hours on the driving range. They have specific skills to learn—the grip, the swing, the correct club to choose. For communicating effectively and to foster that sense of relatedness, we must also learn the basic and specific language skills that will improve our performance. And of course, like the golfer, we can up our communications game with practice.

I was coaching Jim, an outgoing and likeable partner in a law firm. He was struggling with balancing his role as partner and team leader with his self-perception of being a personable guy next door who gets along with everyone. Before becoming an attorney, Jim had been a college athlete. He now coaches competitive youth teams and serves in a leadership role for a national college sports association. He sprinkles sports analogies and game lingo throughout his speech and is perhaps more comfortable on the field than in a conference room. Jim found it challenging to communicate with members of his team who did not share his sports enthusiasm and collegiate style. They did not appreciate the friendly pats on the back that Jim occasionally imposed, as athletes might exchange in a huddle, and did not relate well to the sports analogies Jim used in communicating priorities and delegating tasks. We worked a lot on awareness of his own personal style and those of his team members to enable him to adjust his style to better match those with whom he was communicating.

I shadowed Jim in meetings and observed various exchanges between him and his team. Later, I provided feedback and observations of others' reactions to his specific parlance so Jim could reflect on what was said, how it was said, with whom, and others' reactions. We revisited the situations, rephrased statements, and role-played as the colleagues listening to him, all to put Jim in their shoes as receivers of his message. He began to check himself when he spoke, reducing the use of sports analogies in meetings, replacing them with more widely accepted speech, and using them only on occasion with certain employees who he knew shared his passion for competition and athletics. He started asking about the interests of the other team members and tried to relate to those individuals in areas of their own interests, thereby establishing a rapport that enabled him to converse casually and connect on a more personal level. Jim developed an awareness of his own and others' speaking patterns, and although deliberately choosing his words, he was becoming more aware in the moment and honed his communication style to more effectively connect with his team. It became more natural the more he did so.

Just as the golfer must be aware of where he is in the game—is he in the sand trap, is the wind kicking up, does he have the right club—and the pianist must be aware of each movement in the piece, its key and time signature, awareness is critical for us as communicators. Our perceptions and behaviors create a reality in our brain that may or may not match what others experience as reality. We must be aware of our perceptions, our language and patterns of speech, and what our brain is doing. In the next section we explore what occurs inside the brain during communications.

The Brain, Language, and Communications

From the field of cognitive psychology, we know that dozens of biases exist that cloud our judgment and drive us to erroneous conclusions. In the absence of time, we cannot do a full analysis while in any given situation, so we rely on mental shortcuts, or heuristics (rules of thumb). Our reliance on heuristics is adaptive and helps us manage volumes of data constantly bombarding our senses. Without time to thoroughly evaluate and objectively review all information, our brains use cognitive shortcuts to guide our behavior, attitudes, and even our actions. However, accuracy does not always prevail. Mental bias often leads to errors in memory and judgment.

Psychologists describe cognitive bias as the very basic statistical, judgment, and memory errors that are common to all human beings. Two prominent researchers, Amos Tversky and Daniel Kahneman, put forth a large body of work identifying dozens of cognitive biases.[7] A few of these biases directly impact communications:

- negativity bias

- attentional bias

- bias blind spot

Kahneman's work describes the human tendency to pay more attention, remember, frequently recall, and become aroused by negative, rather than positive, experiences and information. This is called the *negativity bias*. Applied to communications, its key lesson is to avoid negative language in communications. Listeners will remember, attend to, and dwell on the negative words and statements you say, regardless of the amount or frequency of positive words and statements shared. A misstep in our language has considerable consequences for a conversation. Being aware of our language, choosing our words carefully, and avoiding negative statements are specific actions we must take to become better communicators. In coaching, we call these *poison words and phrases*.[8] They tend to derail or kill meaningful and positive conversation. Here are a few examples of poison words and phrases to avoid:

- ✗ Don't feel that way.

- ✗ I told you . . .

- ✗ Always/Never . . .

- ✗ You know . . .

- ✗ But/However (avoid conditions) . . .

- ✗ You need to . . .

✗ You should . . .

Because of negativity bias, our brains will dwell on the poisons despite any positives shared in the same breath. Simply avoiding these can improve your ability to communicate effectively. Avoiding these negative patterns in our speech is not simple. It takes awareness and practice to catch ourselves before we utter them.

Kahneman also identified *attentional bias*—the tendency to pay attention to emotionally charged stimuli in one's environment and to neglect relevant data. When our emotions are involved or when other people touch on a sore spot or push our buttons, our ability to attend to other and perhaps more important or relevant information is severely diminished. It takes real effort to recognize emotionally charged information, identify and ignore triggers, and train ourselves to not overreact to these occurrences. In doing so, however, we can better allow the real content to come through without succumbing to our tendency to get stuck on the emotionally charged content. It is also likely that the communicator is unaware of their use of a poison phrase or emotionally charged content. While they have moved along with the conversation, you may be stuck and stalled several sentences back. By employing a mindfulness practice, in which we identify, name, and acknowledge the elicited emotion, we can observe the emotionally charged thought and then let it go, enabling us to resume participation in the conversation.

We also have a *bias blind spot*. We tend to see ourselves as less biased than other people. We can often identify a bias in someone else but fail to see our own biases, though we all have them. Recognizing these and being aware of how they interfere in our interactions with others can aid us in smoothing the communications pathway. It helps to acknowledge our biases and articulate them. Awareness gives us *and* the other person a chance to modify our reaction and actions.

Bias is rampant in the workplace yet often goes unnoticed by the biased individual. A client of mine named Janet, a team leader in a small firm, discovered her own bias during the coaching process. Through the restructuring of teams due to a need for more support on a large project, she acquired two new team members who had been hired and trained by one of her peers before their assignment to Janet's project. Up to that point, Janet had personally interviewed, selected, and trained her own team members. She identified a need for additional resources, hoping to get a few more open positions approved for hire. Instead, her management realigned existing staff and moved two current employees to her team. They had functioned in a similar capacity on another team and were both qualified and competent in the work Janet's team was doing.

In coaching, Janet articulated her frustration in managing the disparate team and cited particular challenges associated with the two new analysts. Still fuming over the denial of her request to hire additional staff, Janet allowed her resentment of her boss's decision to interfere with her ability to discern and cultivate the talent she had been given. Her bias prevented her from seeing the contributions these two were making and hindered her own success as a leader when she did not empower them to fully utilize their skills. Once she recognized her bias and opened herself to the possibility that the two new analysts could be an asset, she was better able to lead and integrate the entire team, taking advantage of the additional resources they had to offer.

There are other pitfalls beside bias that impede our judgment.

Framing, in the social sciences, refers to a set of concepts and perspectives on how we organize, perceive, and communicate about reality. Your reality is different from mine based on how we frame a situation. We interpret information based on the framework we apply. For example, our reactions to "We are 90 percent likely to close the sale" versus "We have a 10 percent chance of losing the client" differ because of the contextual frame applied. The former boasts an optimistic perspective; the latter is framed in failure.

Each of us also use and rely on a *schema of interpretation,* a unique collection of anecdotes and stereotypes, to understand the world and respond to events.[9] We build our own sets of mental filters to make sense of the world. Choices we then make are influenced by our creation of a framework through which we interpret the world. This mental shortcut does not always yield desired results; it is seen more as a rule of thumb. According to Susan T. Fiske and Shelley E. Taylor, human beings are by nature "cognitive misers," meaning they prefer to do as little thinking as possible.[10] In our efforts to conserve mental energy, we fall victim to errors and poor decision-making influenced by the schema of interpretation we impose on our own realities. In clinical settings, cognitive behavioral therapy (CBT) and dialectical behavioral therapy (DBT) involve learning new ways to frame situations so dysfunctional thinking and behavior are minimized.

Good communicators can benefit by being aware of their own framing biases and schema. They learn to reframe situations, allowing communications to be more fruitful. In experiencing conversations, our behavior and thoughts are often significantly guided by prior situations and earlier similar conversations. This is particularly true in emotionally charged or important conversations.

In the workplace, one of the most emotionally charged conversations is a performance review. While many companies have a formal structure to be followed in reviewing performance, the conversation between the reviewer and the employee is not scripted. The discussion is subject to considerable framing errors and the application of schema and preconceived expectations. Your reviewer may be fatigued from having already done six reviews this month and has inadvertently categorized his employees as "good performers" and "poor performers" in his mind. Going into your review, he carries a frame, or schema, into the conversation. His actions are guided by the frame and schema his brain has already applied. For a poor performer, he expects to discuss your past mistakes and present his plan for your additional training to avoid them in the future. He anticipates you might be defiant, apathetic, or lazy. He prepared for the meeting with this in mind. He expects you might object or offer excuses, so he has prepared justifications and examples and is eager to conclude the meeting after conveying the news that you will not receive a pay increase. He wants to keep it short and simple and stick to the facts. This could be his poor-performer-review schema. While it may be useful in some review situations, it is inadequate for many real situations.

What if John, a poor performer, came into the review with earnest acknowledgment of the earlier mistakes he had made? What if he agreed his work was not acceptable and shared that he had been having some personal problems that he allowed to interfere with his work? John shares that he has made changes outside of work that enable him to better focus on his job, and he intends to work extra hours to compensate for his earlier poor performance. He asks if he could receive additional help in some areas to better understand what's expected and is willing to study after hours to gain the required knowledge. John, it appears, does not fit well into his reviewer's preconceived notion of poor performer, and the schema is no longer a reliable guide. While the reviewer had hoped to get by with little cognitive effort in exercising this review, his schema is not appropriate in this case. He cannot rely on this mental shortcut; he must deliberately and thoughtfully redirect his thinking and actions.

Negativity Bias Exercise

One way to reduce or eliminate negativity in your language is to role-play an important conversation in advance.

1. Identify an important conversation to use for this exercise. Practice speaking what you plan to say.

2. Ask someone else to act as the listener, or you can respond as a listener yourself.

3. Record the role-play on your phone or computer.

4. Play back the recording. Count the instances in which you use poison words and phrases.

5. For each instance of the poison words and phrase, think of an alternative way to say it and write it down.

6. Repeat the role play until you have eliminated the poison words.

7. In the real situation, you may not remember all your alternative

words, but your awareness and ability to correct yourself will have improved.

Antidote for Poison Bias Exercise

Most of us have some awareness of our own biases and patterns of speech. Eliminating poison phrases from our conversations greatly improves our success as communicators. Awareness of our common go-to habits in conversations is the basis of creating change, so it is helpful to first articulate these so we can then work on better alternatives. Using the example chart below, create your own Poison Phrase Awareness Grid as follows:

1. Thinking about your common behaviors during interactions with peers, friends, coworkers, and family, write down a list of the poison phrases you are currently aware of in your recent communications repertoire.

2. Give an example of each.

3. For each example, write down an alternative way of communicating in that situation that could be more effective. This is the antidote alternative to be used instead of a poison phrase.

4. Complete the Poison Phrase Awareness Grid below with your examples:

Poison phrase	Your example	More positive alternative
Always/Never		
You should		
Don't feel that way		
I told you		
You know . . .		
I know . . .		
But/However		
You need to . . .		

Here is an example of the Poison Phrase Awareness Grid filled out.

Poison phrase	Example	Alternative
Always/Never	You never listen to me when I talk.	I'm frustrated when I think you are not listening.
You should	You should turn off the computer when we are talking.	Can we go somewhere quiet to talk?

CHAPTER 4
Upping Your Communications Game

In learning any new skill, we continue to refine techniques as we approach mastery. The golfer gets better when she learns the mechanics of a good swing and must continually refine and practice until the swing becomes second nature. Her repeated behavior for the stance, grip, and glance toward the hole establish patterns that can improve or hinder her game. In communications, we also have behaviors that can hinder or foster mastery. By becoming aware of maladaptive patterns in our ways of speaking, we can then check and correct ourselves, choosing more effective ways of expression that hone our messages masterfully. We can up our communication game by using constructive techniques and eliminating bad habits.

Language Patterns

Some frequently used language patterns serve only to inhibit communications by shutting down a dialogue or seriously limiting how we think about options and possibilities.[11] When speaking, it is best to avoid the types of inhibitors listed in figure 4.1.

Figure 4.1: Language inhibitors

Inhibitor	Example
Deletion (not providing enough information)	I had to leave.
Ambiguity	She hates me.
Generalization	
Always/Never	My boss never puts me on the good projects. My coworker always comes in late.
Necessity	I need to work late to get the promotion.
Possibility	I can't do Excel.
Distortion	
Mind Reading	You don't care that my car broke down.
Cause and Effect	She didn't do her share of the work just so I'd have to scramble to complete our project.
Presumption	I didn't get the promotion. It must mean the boss doesn't like me.

In *deletion,* we intentionally omit pertinent details. We are stingy with information. Rather than just offering "I had to leave," telling your boss "I had to leave unexpectedly because of a family emergency" imparts information and opens the possibility of empathy. "She hates me" provides little insight into her feelings, but "She and I disagree over the projected budget" leaves room for further discussion and possible resolution by avoiding use of *ambiguity,* or vague verbs. *Generalizing,* in its various forms, serves to lessen the impact and credibility of your statements. *Always* and *never* denote hard absolutes, which in most cases are simply not true. And they convey static conditions without possibility of change. Hope for change is a powerful motivator, and anything we can do in conversation to foster hope and possibility is a positive and powerful tool. No one likes to be pigeonholed.

Necessity is seldom motivating. The very word conjures up images of drudgery, coercion, or worse. Do you really need to work late to get the promotion, or do you want to show you are dedicated to the job and position yourself for promotion? If you want something, it is so much more likely you will work for it and feel better about working for it than if you are forced or feel obligated to do so. Let your language reflect this. Repeated use of necessity statements guide your framing in a negative direction. If you often say "I need to work late," you may come to resent your job and your boss and abandon aspirations for that promotion you sought. Rephrasing it to "I am working late because I want to be considered for the supervisor role" is forward thinking, positive, and motivating. It places emphasis on what you want rather than what you might feel obligated to do.

We often sabotage ourselves when we eliminate *possibility* with words like *can't*. At work, retraining or learning new skills is sometimes necessary simply to maintain one's current job. Frustration and denigration of our own abilities is common. By stating, for example, "I can't do Excel," you limit your own possibilities and disparage your abilities. With training or practice, perhaps you *can* "do Excel." Or perhaps someone on your team can help out with skills not in your toolbox. Restating it to something like "The spreadsheet could be made into a nice chart, but I'm not yet proficient enough in Excel to do it" leaves the opportunity for someone else to help out or for you to get the training you need. The negative suddenly becomes more positive by simply stating the idea in more positive and less restrictive language. Furthermore, skilled use of positive language can regard a situation as temporary, which can be rectified, instilling hope and forward thinking.

Distortion language results from inferences we make about the intentions of others. While we can observe behavior, we can't observe others' thoughts. We tend to assume the worst about someone's intentions when things aren't going our way. We are better off asking for clarification than *mind reading,* inferring a *cause* and *effect,* or making assumptions. We would do better to state our own thoughts and feelings and let the other person clarify theirs, even if their behavior is confusing. In the case of mind reading, "You won't care that my car broke down" distorts reality because in reality, we cannot know what another person is thinking. They may care, but by stating "You won't care," we present something as fact and put the other person on the defensive.

We humans love to attribute motives to others' behavior. Our brains tend to attribute cause and effect when causes are unclear or especially when the outcome negatively affects us. How likely is it that he didn't do his part of the project just to make things difficult for you? If he didn't do his share of the group project, could it be because he was called away to pick up a sick child from school? Or the work took longer than he had anticipated and while he did start the work, he was unable to finish? Perhaps he didn't have the knowledge or skill to finish? Assuming he intended for you to scramble is but one of myriad possibilities. Stating your perceived view of a negative intention does nothing more than brew animosity. Instead, ask him directly what happened to impact his part. "How did it go with your part of the project?" opens the door of possibility and reduces a negative effect by inviting an explanation from the source.

Like mind reading and cause and effect, *presumptions* also inhibit good communication. Deriving meaning from an action without consulting the source inhibits real learning, shutting down information gathering. You could ask the boss what you could have done to get the promotion or what credentials the chosen candidate had that led to their receipt of an offer and your rejection. If you presume the boss dislikes you, it may negatively influence your actions toward them in future interactions. It is always better to get meaningful information from the source than to presume.

As you can see, language inhibitors rob us of the chance for understanding, clarity, and meaningful insights. And these patterns can accumulate and build up to affect our overall outlook in a negative way. Being careful to reduce and remove these maladaptive language inhibitors from our communication will pave the way for a more positive outlook and better communication.

Communications Styles

Coaches spend a great deal of effort on developing clients' awareness of behaviors, attitudes, patterns, and frameworks—that is, how we perceive or experience events in terms of what we already know or have experienced. In spoken language, we each have a unique voice and style of communicating, though some common styles exist that can hinder or enhance communication. It is helpful to be cognizant of stylistic language we use, and as with awareness of any behavior, it is the fundamental basis of change. Only when we are aware of our language patterns can we make a conscious decision to choose different patterns in an effort to improve communications. Consider how differently we construct texts versus emails. It exemplifies how stylistic patterns can enhance or hinder communications. We tend to be more formal in email than texts and use more slang in texts than emails. How you text your boss should differ from how you text your best friend. Use of slang, emojis, and grammatical liberties are acceptable perhaps in an email to the guys about Saturday's pickup game but not so much in an email to your child's teacher or your colleague, legislator, or attorney. When we begin to notice and acknowledge the stylistic patterns of communication, we can then discern more appropriate patterns to use in our own communciations.

Schemas, as discussed with the performance review scenario in chapter 3, often guide our internal frameworks of thought or behavior in interpreting our world. Schemas are persistent and help us categorize and classify experience without spending too much brain energy. Our perception is driven by schemas. We have schemas for common experiences, such as taking the bus, going to a restaurant, attending a meeting, going on a date, and participating in team sports. They help us categorize and organize our behaviors and thoughts so we don't have to reinvent the wheel each time we encounter a situation. Many forms of therapy today involve development of awareness of the client's own schemas, and in understanding these we can then work to change those schemas if necessary or at least be cognizant of their power on our ability to interpret, or perhaps misinterpret, our world. Schemas also influence our communication by framing our speech in predetermined patterns.

Communication Schemas

In language, schemas are frameworks that direct our communications in ways that either hinder or enhance our message, color it with hope or pessimism, empower or inhibit growth. Coaching has a forward focus. When clients present with communication challenges to overcome, we often begin by exploring the various communications styles they may use and bringing awareness to the implications of using our go-to frameworks in expressing ourselves. Some styles tend to draw in the listener while others repel and present barriers to understanding. These various styles of speech can open possibilities while others shut down communication with stifling finality:

- ✓ toward versus away

- ✓ internal versus external

- ✓ proactive versus reactive

- ✓ detailed versus global

- ✓ same versus different

- ✓ options versus procedure

Using a *toward* versus *away* style could tip the scale in a more positive, growth-oriented direction. An away style is less proactive and contains an avoidance perspective that tells what the speaker is moving away from. This works against the growth and forward focus in which communication thrives. Listeners prefer to hear about approach rather than avoidance behaviors. The toward style in language supports individual accountability and intention. "I want to develop a career" conjures up images of a person working toward something constructive. The away style (for example, "I don't want a minimum-wage job") gives little clue as to the speaker's intended action, only highlighting what is to be avoided. Whenever possible, speak with a toward style to engage the listener with an action-oriented, forward-moving growth mindset.

An *internal* style brings the focus of a statement and accountability to the speaker. Internal style is where the speaker owns the behavior, taking pride and claiming responsibility for a particular quality or act. No communication benefits from accusatory statements or placing blame. In claiming ownership, we allow for possibilities and eliminate the limiting, static judgments of others. In an internal style (for example, "I find it difficult to work with him"), we allow for a change in the situation. Maybe I can do something to make it easier to work with him; maybe it is my bias, ignorance, or inability that is getting in the way. Conversely, "He is hard to work with" implies finality and passes judgment, allows little room for discussion or problem-solving, and puts the onus on him and not the speaker. If the speaker wants to keep a forward focus, the internal style invites options and possibilities of devising ways to better work together. Focusing on our own difficulty in working with others puts the onus on us and our challenges, which can be viewed as a temporary thing that can be fixed, rather than claiming inherent failings in others.

To use external focus inhibits our own ability to exercise our power over challenges. We often see this concept expressed with the advice of using "I" statements in positive interpersonal communications. This helps keep us from using accusatory "you" statements and placing blame on others, allowing us to claim responsibility for our own feelings and thoughts.

Similarly, switching from a *reactive* to *proactive* style places the responsibility on the speaker, empowering them to take action in a constructive manner. Reactive statements, such as "I'll correct the report if the boss finds any errors," victimize the speaker, offering little chance of exerting control over a situation. Proactive style empowers the speaker, implying action and behavior, as in the example "I am double-checking my report."

Speaking with a *detailed* style is much more tangible than a global one. Providing details allows for specific and even measurable opportunity. Using *global* references, however, provides too little information to the listener. Global style can be ambiguous and is generally not actionable. For example, "I want to do better marketing" does not make it clear to the listener what better marketing entails. The specific action of "establishing a Facebook page" is an idea a listener can more easily understand. While global style is acceptable in certain situations, such as when soliciting ideas from a group or in brainstorming sessions to generate options, it is important to recognize when speaking in a detail-oriented style would be more effective.

While *same/different* schemas may or may not be problematic in speech, it is important to recognize when we are using same or different contexts because they are also schemas that may shortchange real understanding. Sometimes calling attention to differences does little to foster collaboration and problem-solving and serves only to divide. Awareness of our use of these styles is helpful in creating fruitful communication. The statement "He and I work best in groups" calls attention to something both people have in common. Placing emphasis on differences such as "He doesn't like group projects like I do" could be viewed as divisive and by simply stating "I like group projects" instead, you remove any judgment about his preferences.

One of the standard practices in coaching is to encourage a client to generate *options* when faced with challenges. Many ways to overcome a challenge can be considered, and by broadening our thinking and coming up with a variety of solutions or means to solutions, we again open up possibility. Too often we tend to jump right into action in resolving issues before considering other, perhaps better, options. Similarly with speech, if we speak in terms of options, we give ourselves a chance to generate and consider multiple or better solutions. Doling out *procedures* and immediately proceding with solutions shuts down discussion and precludes generation of potentially better solutions. While directly establishing procedures is called for in many situations, it often results from first having generated options. If upon discovering a project is behind schedule a team leader declares, "Staff can work an extra ten hours," consideration for other solutions has been eliminated. An alternative statement, "One option is to reallocate resources," opens up possibilities and invites options. Knowing when each communication style is appropriate requires an awareness of when and how best to use them. In the last example the immediate solution of changing procedures to require staff to work an additional ten hours is bound to be unpopular, particularly if other options were not first discussed.

Though we may use the various speech styles at times, it is important to be aware of them and how they influence our ability to communicate effectively and constructively. By recognizing which of these you use, you will be empowered to choose a more meaningful and effective way of communicating. It takes practice to catch ourselves using these patterns. If we are on the alert, we are likely to recognize potential pitfalls and avoid using schemas and styles that inhibit understanding. Self-awareness of our own behaviors (and speech) and knowing where we are and what we are thinking in the moment is the first step toward growth and transformation. Then when we learn more effective language skills, we become even better communicators.

There are countless ways our use of language influences communication. Self-awareness and awareness of others is paramount for being in the moment and present for an ultimate interaction. Be cognizant of your emotions and those of others, where you are and where they are at that moment, the many cognitive biases we all have, your language patterns and inhibitors, and schemas applied during a conversation. Consider how what you say and how you say it can either frustrate or fulfill your psychological needs and those of others.

Language Inhibitor Exercise

All of us use the common language inhibitors, styles, and schemas to some degree. Again, awareness of our own styles is the first step in improving communications. Using the example grid below, create your own communications style grid as follows:

1. Identify which three language inhibitors from figure 4.1 you use most often.

2. For each of these three, write down an example of when you used that inhibitor.

3. Think of a way to reframe that situation and write down a more positive, appropriate response.

Complete the Language Inhibitors Grid below with your examples.

Language Inhibitor	Example	Alternative
Deletion		
Ambiguity		
Always/Never		
Necessity		
Possibility		
Mind-Reading		
Cause/Effect		
Presumptions		

Here is an example of the Language Inhibitors Grid filled out.

Language Inhibitor	Example	Alternative
Deletion	I couldn't do the conference call—I was busy.	My early meeting ran over, so I was unable to join the conference call. What did I miss?
Necessity	I need to ace this interview.	I want to do my best in the interview because I'm very interested in this job and I want to make it to the next round.

CHAPTER 5
Lion or Lamb:
The Communications Continuum

Communication involves a range of practices that can demonstrate extremes of intensity, respect, and empowerment unless careful attention is paid to tone and demeanor. Speakers may convey power and aggression or appear timid and self-conscious. They may exude respect or disregard. Specific behaviors adopted by speakers can balance the scale for empowered communication that facilitates respect and understanding. This chapter explores the continuum along which communication behavior moves, from passivity to aggression, and ways to manage intensity, respect rights, and drive toward understanding.

What It Means to Be Assertive

Assertive communication is a form of expression that enables your needs to be met while still considering the needs of others. Assertiveness empowers us and the people we communicate with to express needs and ideas in a nonthreatening way. Being assertive is not a natural behavior for most of us; it must be learned and practiced. In fact, communicating assertively may seem uncomfortable at first. Yet there are definite techniques to learn that will improve significantly with practice.

> **Assertive: as-ser-tive [uh-SUR-tiv]**
> To state or to express positively; confidently self-assured; positive

You may have misconceptions about what it means to be assertive. People who communicate assertively are not pushy or obnoxious. They do not step on the feelings of others to get what they want. Rather, assertive communication involves expressing your feelings, needs, and desires in a nonjudgmental and nonthreatening way. To understand assertiveness, it is helpful to look at it in relation to passivity and aggression, as shown in figure 5.1.

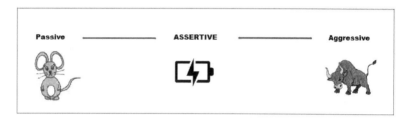

Figure 5.1: Spectrum of passivity/aggression

Think of a continuum of respect, where passivity is on one side, aggression is on the other, and assertiveness is dead center. Assertiveness is an expression of respect for the self and others in a nonthreatening way. Communicating assertively is not selfish but rather helps us effectively navigate within social encounters. It comes down to respecting everyone's rights. With assertive communications, we take ownership for our feelings and do not place blame or infer causality. Consider the following common characteristics of assertive communication style:

✓ expresses one's own needs

✓ considers others' needs

✓ is nonthreatening

✓ exudes respect

✓ takes ownership of feelings

✓ empowers self and others

✓ is not natural—must be learned

✓ requires practice

Assertive communications must be learned as we refine our language skills. Consider our initial language development as small children: It starts off a bit demanding and aggressive. Somewhere between young childhood and adulthood, we learn styles of communicating that tend to fall somewhere along that continuum, often falling closer to passivity or aggression, depending on many factors such as family environment, education, and social experience. While personality researchers might consider passivity a relatively stable characteristic of introverts, social and cognitive psychologists regard it as more of a demonstrated behavior influenced by situational and perceived circumstances, which can be changed with learning and experience.

Passivity in Communications

Passive communication is an ineffective and maladaptive form of expression. Those with a passive communication style may be afraid of confrontation and may not feel they have the right to make their wishes and desires known. It is as if the speaker ignores their own feelings and does not clearly express them. Not only is being a passive communicator ineffective when communicating your message, this style of expression can lead to feelings of anxiety, anger, depression, and helplessness. Consider these common characteristics of passive communication style:

- ✗ is maladaptive and ineffective

- ✗ avoids confrontation

- ✗ involves vague requests

- ✗ fails to assert an opinion

- ✗ feels like one has no right to make one's own wishes known

- ✗ can lead to anxiety, anger, depression, and helplessness

Recall the story of Terence, from the introduction, who was dissatisfied with his wage increase and performance review. While Terence left the encounter confused and with unresolved questions, his choice to not challenge the boss at that moment is understandable. Terence may have been caught off guard, not expecting the meager increase, and was better off expressing his needs at a separate time. In calling the subsequent meeting with his boss, Terence was soon able to express himself in a constructive, clear, factual, and nonthreatening manner—in short, assertively.

Passive communication usually involves vague requests for help, similarly unclear references, and wishing rather than requesting directly. Even not expressing an opinion can be considered passive if needs are never expressed. Waiting to express an opinion until you can do so constructively is not passive. Take time to craft your response to avoid threatening, judgmental, or reactive behavior.

Consider the following statements:

Passive: "I am concerned I will not meet the deadline given the number of hours left to complete the work."

Assertive: "What can be done to extend the deadline or get more help to complete the work?"

The former expresses the idea that the speaker is behind schedule, but the latter is much more actionable and specific in soliciting the listener's solution to the problem presented. The former is a bit vague, and the listener could simply acknowledge concern without offering any solution. The latter directly engages the listener in coming up with a solution. The former uses a passive communication style and understates the speaker's needs, whereas the latter is assertive and addresses the need. No one's feelings were attacked, no blame was levied—just a clear request for ideas to get the work done was offered. That is assertive communication. Here's another example:

Passive: "I wish the deadline for this project was next month."

Assertive: "I am requesting to move the deadline to next month."

We can almost envision a little mouse or lamb shrinking away and softly muttering under their breath, wishing for change. Compare that image with a fully charged battery, an action cell, that lays out the direct request: move the deadline. It is easy to see how the assertive statement is more effective—the call to action is clear, there are no vague references. Wishing often doesn't lead to desired results and, as with nonassertive communication styles, can lead to unwanted outcomes.

Aggression Interferes with Communication

On the other end of the expression continuum is the aggressive communication style. Like its polar opposite, the passive style, the aggressive form is also maladaptive and ineffective. It ignores others' feelings, can be seen as a verbal attack, and imparts a feeling that the aggressor intends to cause harm. The speaker using an aggressive style is often perceived as bullying, vengeful, uncompromising, and selfish. This hardly sets up a receptive audience. Aggressive communication involves verbal attacks rather than expressing a need. It tends to put others on the defensive. It does not foster cooperation or problem-solving. Consider these common characteristics of aggressive communication style:

✗ is maladaptive and ineffective

✗ disregards others' feelings

✗ involves verbal attacks

✗ is perceived as bullying, rigid, selfish

✗ implies intent to harm

✗ works against compromise and problem-resolution

Consider the statements below:

Aggressive: "You screwed up the project."

Assertive: "The project issues require correction."

Both statements clearly indicate a problem with the project. However, there is a way to communicate this without placing blame, by recognizing the facts without degrading the other person. The two statements illustrate subtle yet powerful differences in their ability to facilitate communication, forward thinking, and problem-solving. In the workplace, the latter example opens the door to constructive resolution, examining issues with the project and cooperative efforts to rectify. Demoralizing the listener, as in the former statement, serves only to shut down possibilities and hamper any desired results while detracting from the speaker's overall demeanor. It evokes images of an angry bull in the bullring or a lion roaring at its prey. The assertive alternative, however, invites resolution.

Communicating in a Mixed Style

Another common style combines qualities of both aggression and passivity: the *passive-aggressive* style. It involves being indirectly aggressive. A speaker using a passive-aggressive communication style often does the following:

✗ acts indirectly aggressive

✗ resists requests

✗ welcomes procrastination

✗ embodies a cold shoulder or sullenness

✗ responds with sarcasm

✗ employs contradictory verbal and nonverbal responses

✗ alters timing by withholding expression followed by a blast of emotion

Passive-aggressive behavior may manifest itself in several different ways. For example, a person might repeatedly make excuses to avoid certain people as a way of expressing their dislike or anger toward those individuals. Often what is intended not to cause harm ultimately does due to a delayed, pent-up reaction. In communication, sarcasm is a common form of passive-aggressiveness. Teenagers' mantra "Whatever!" is really sarcasm. Another form is martyrdom. Rather than expressing displeasure directly, invoking guilt in another is passive-aggressive communication. Often passive-aggressiveness involves an issue of timing. Initially, the speaker suppresses their thoughts, only to explode later, first ignoring their own feelings and later ignoring others'.

Assertive expression can be used in place of all these ineffective styles. This manner of communication respects everyone's rights and feelings, both the speaker's and the listener's (see figure 5.2).

Figure 5.2: Expressive styles and rights

Passive	Violates one's own rights; disregards self
Passive-Aggressive	Violates everyone's rights; initially disregards self, then later disregards others
Aggressive	Violates others' rights; disregards others
Assertive	Respects everyone's rights

Assertive communication can also be considered helpful to others because you are giving clear information about what you need to be satisfied. By doing so in a nonthreatening manner, you also give others the opportunity to refuse your requests if your needs conflict with their needs.

Techniques for Communicating Assertively

Now that we know why speaking assertively is good for our own communications and for those with whom we communicate, it is important to learn specific techniques for putting assertiveness into practice.

Breathe and Relax

We often minimize the importance of breathing, and many people are not aware of how they breathe and how breathing affects behavior. Tension and anxiety work against assertive communication, and deep breathing allows us to relax and positions us for more effective expression. Stress reduction, meditation, and yoga all rely heavily on breathing as a foundation for their practice, but there are dozens of times throughout a day when deliberate breathing can benefit us. Long, deep breaths, in which we engage our diaphragm muscle to expand and contract the rib cage, promote relaxation. Breathing this way is controlled and deliberate and must be practiced to become second nature. In our busy, intense world, so often we resort to hurried, shallow breaths without even being aware of it. Our culture glorifies a flat belly, and many concerned with body image constantly hold in their stomach, preventing deep breathing. So to be fully positioned for assertive communication, practice slow, deliberate, deep breathing.

Be aware of every breath in and every breath out. Breathe in through the nose and push the air out and exhale through the mouth to fully inflate and empty the lungs. Feel the belly rise, not the shoulders. Really concentrate on your breath. Some people find it helpful to close their eyes, repeat a phrase or word in their mind, or use imagery to promote relaxed breathing. This concentrated form of breathing also tends to remove or redirect attention away from distractions in our environment. Ten or twelve cycles of long inhales and pushed exhales are enough to allow your tension to lessen and your muscles to relax. Deep, slow breathing has been shown to suppress the fight-or-flight reflex, the stress response from the sympathetic nervous system. It can lower blood pressure and decrease the heart rate. Try practicing this for a few minutes daily until you can readily activate deep breathing. When you are in a communication situation, you can invoke deep breathing to position yourself for a relaxed interaction.

Use "I" Statements

Assertive communication in practice requires that we own and take responsibility for our communication. Statements beginning with "I" enable us to state our thoughts, needs, and observations. Just as we saw with poison words, statements beginning with "you" tend to be accusatory and presumptuous. They cause the listener to begin thinking of ways to counter our statements in their own defense.

A helpful sentence construct is "I feel . . . when this happens . . . because . . . ."

It is crucial to recognize that your thoughts and feelings are important and in stating them, you honor and respect yourself. Using "I" statements allows this while not disrespecting the rights of the listener. It takes practice, as we tend to react with "you" statements, as young children often demonstrate in communicating their dissatisfaction and needs. If you have an important conversation, some bit of advance preparation is helpful. Think about the "I" statements to use, check yourself if you begin to think in terms of "you," and consider what points you want to convey.

In coaching clients for assertive communication, I often use role-playing to practice using "I" statements. The clients approach the conversation while I act as the listener. I respond as would a listener, depending on how clients articulate their thoughts. If they stray from using "I" statements, I start using defensive language and we examine and discuss how the conversation became derailed. We repeat the role play many times, as needed, to hone the language skills and bring awareness to the various language barriers and boosters. Feedback is key to developing self-awareness in clients. This gives them a way to practice formulating language in constructive ways and an opportunity to articulate important points. Feedback and iterative role play allow empowering speech patterns to develop, all before the real conversation takes place.

Even without a coach, you can coach yourself on these practices by thinking about an upcoming interaction in advance, formulating your "I" statements, practicing the deep and slow breathing technique, and speaking in front of a mirror. Today, technology also provides readily available means for practice. For example, record in your own voice your planned statements on a mobile device recorder and then listen to the playback. Or record yourself in a video. Listen for inadvertent "you" statements and then rephrase them in terms of "I" statements. Use technology's voice recorders and film capabilities to promote self-awareness, affirm self-image, and introduce repetition in developing new habits.

Focus on the Solution

In heated, or even neutral, discussions, it is so easy to get off topic and go off on tangents. To optimize assertive communications, think about the point of the interaction and direct all conversations toward that point. Try to solve one thing at a time, don't allow yourself or others to wander away from the topic at hand until it is resolved. It takes discipline to remain focused. But by doing so, you and others will reap the benefit of having achieved or at least advanced the desired understanding. Sometimes the origin of a challenge is less important in resolution than executing a plan, conveying information, or airing concerns that need to be addressed. Don't waste time on those less important detractors and instead spend the effort and energy on what matters. Keep the interaction forward focused, as if you are moving toward a desired end state. Conversations that continually rehash aired grievances become tedious, with participants losing interest and tolerance quickly. If you suspect this is happening, quickly move on and perhaps even acknowledge the lack of progress and take a break.

With a forward, solution-based focus, it is necessary to keep things short and simple. Embellishing, elaborating, and droning on work against assertive communication. These tactics detract from your message. The famous KISS principle works wonders for assertive communications: Keep It Short and Simple.

Ask Questions

Unless you are giving a speech, communication is rarely one-directional. If more than one person is involved, questions must be asked. Fact finding is necessary, clarification is crucial, and through questions we can begin to tease out important and contributing factors that influence the listeners. Shooting a barrage of inquiries is not effective however. The type of questions matter. There are ways to inquire that will elicit meaning and real information—these are open-ended questions. Simple yes-or-no questions contribute little and may be considered annoying. Open-ended queries allow more content to be conveyed, offer alternate considerations, and promote the forward focus. They sometimes start with how or what and generate alternative perspectives, solutions, and ideas.

Here are a few examples of open-ended questions:

- What else can I do to assist you?

- What further information can I provide for you?

- How can we resolve the issue?

Questions can help us understand even when a speaker is not using assertive communications. There are definite dos and don'ts in language that promote versus hinder.

One great technique for better understanding is to incorporate some of the following power words and expressions into your everyday conversations:

✓ It seems you feel . . .

✓ It seems you think . . .

✓ Let's look at options.

✓ What do you think?

✓ What you are saying makes sense.

✓ Given [the situation], what would work?

Can you feel your mind expanding when you say these? Can you feel how you are empowering yourself and others? Can you feel how nonthreatening it is? These expressions set a neutral perspective and can take the heat out of an especially intense interchange.

Just as positive emotion is generated from connected communications with others, positive language comes from deliberate word choices. The power words in figure 5.3 act to open up a dialogue, expand our thinking, and invite possibilities.

Figure 5.3: Power words for positive language

Practice sprinkling these positive words throughout your conversation and use them in place of negative choices or poison words. As we discussed with the negativity bias, our brains will pay acute attention to the negative more so than any positive words. Avoid the poison words and expressions that detract from a neutral, open-minded, or solution-focused exchange.

Whereas the power words empower and expand communication possibilities, poison words, discussed in chapter 3, shut down communications. We also react physically when we hear them. We tense up, our heart rate increases, our breathing becomes shallower, and blood pressure can increase. Treat these words as poison and remove them from your language.

It is so important to avoid verbal attacks and accusations. Often assertive communication becomes especially challenging when discussing a problem that the other person caused. In these situations, it is easy to point fingers, but remember to keep things forward focused. Once the grievance is aired, it is best to leave an option for that person to save face and rectify the situation. Keeping to direct observations and facts allows the other person to draw their own conclusions and consider options rather than putting them on the defensive. You might find that you want the other person to know how their actions affected you. This can be stated by using the "I" statements so you are respecting your own needs, and then simply move on to the solution focus. Stick to the topic. Keep a separate list (known as a "parking lot") of issues to return to at a later time.

This enables you to acknowledge concerns while not letting them get in the way of what you came to discuss and the topic at hand. The other person may digress into tangential subjects, and it becomes necessary to steer the conversation back on target. You can even say, "That is a good point, which we will come back to . . . ." Endeavor to be less confrontational.

As a management consultant, I frequently conduct or participate in meetings with stakeholders, administrators, and vendors. Once I was in a meeting with a healthcare system administrator, Elliot, and the system vendor to resolve software deficiencies in a product that was currently being implemented at the hospital. The organization's facilitator, to keep the meeting running efficiently and within allocated time limits, used a system of waving color-coded cards to indicate if participants were moving away from the topic at hand (red stop sign) or becoming confrontational (yellow traffic light). While the facilitator's intentions were noble, the execution of this card-waving spectacle completely detracted from the purpose of constructive information gathering and problem resolution, and it unfortunately irritated participants, inciting animosity and frustration among the group. The red cards virtually became a stop sign. Imagine, while speaking, how distracting it would be to be interrupted with a stop sign waved vehemently by a moderator across the table. Elliot did not appreciate this form of meeting management. He perceived it as passive aggression and became less inclined to share his concerns and contribute potential solutions. Instead of using signs, the facilitator could have made use of a whiteboard to note any tangential issues to return to at a later point (the parking-lot approach). And the facilitator could also have used assertive communication to tactfully state when a comment was not directly related to the problem and would be noted for later discussion instead of the card-waving system, which eroded trust.

Outside of meetings, there are plenty of problem situations in which we can use nonconfrontational communication toward resolution. Consider the examples in figure 5.4.

Figure 5.4: Nonconfrontational alternatives

Original: You're in my seat! **Better:** It looks like we have the same assigned seat.
Original: You scheduled a meeting for the end of the day! **Better:** I realize we are meeting at 4 p.m. today, and I want you to know that since today is my day for carpool, I must leave promptly at 4:30. If we are not finished by then I can arrange to come in early tomorrow morning to resume our discussion, or if you'd prefer, we can start at 3:30 to give us more time.
Original: You never submitted the report. **Better:** I am having difficulty locating the paperwork.
Original: I can't do Excel. **Better:** I would like more training in Excel so I can better forecast the budget.
Original: That's not relevant today. **Better:** That's a point I hadn't considered. Let's add it to the agenda for Thursday's follow-up meeting.

Being direct is okay. In fact, being direct is a prerequisite for assertive communication. The simple lesson is to ask for what you want and state your feelings. We simply cannot rely on other people somehow just knowing what we want. We have the responsibility of telling them in a nonconfrontational way. Use direct language—no beating around the bush. It is good to slow down the pace of an exchange to give yourself time to think about what you want to say and how to say it in a positive manner. Don't cushion the message or couch it in fluff. There is no need to go into elaborate preface. Using clear observations and facts, ask for what you want slowly, simply, and specifically. Allow the other person time to reflect, too, and if necessary, resume the discussion later. To hasten into a resolution or insist on closure prematurely may yield a less than ideal outcome. Take and give the time needed.

Choosing direct language, however, is sometimes difficult given traditional gender stereotypes and norms. Historically, women especially were often viewed as aggressive if they expressed themselves in a direct and assertive manor. Workplace research consistently indicates that women who behave assertively by emphasizing their skills, accomplishments, expertise, or goals may be seen as competent, but at the same time they incur the risk of being perceived as unlikeable, not team players or leaders, abrasive, or shrill. And women often are aware of being negatively received when acting assertively, causing them to modify their behaviors in less assertive ways. In doing so, they are less successful in negotiating business deals, obtaining promotions or raises, or expressing competence in the workplace.[12] Other studies show that tempering assertive communications with politeness and cultural sensitivity can be useful in communicating effectively while maintaining the respect-all mantra of assertive communication. Though women studied did acknowledge the effectiveness of this approach, they noted that male counterparts did not have to exert the extra efforts to read the situation and modify their communication styles accordingly.[13]

The demure, other-focused, soft-spoken woman of traditional gender stereotypes has significant challenges from a communication perspective if she is to succeed in the workplace and in personal relationships. Yet still these stereotypes persist. Sheryl Sandberg, in her book Lean In, discusses the idea that even young girls who assert themselves are seen as "bossy" while the boys exhibiting the same behavior are seen as leaders.[14] These role biases are a barrier to clear communication and assertive behavior, and while we must be mindful of these, at the same time we must work to eliminate them and their effects, both as speakers and listeners. And as we so often come back to the idea of awareness as a basis for changing behavior, awareness of these gender biases will allow us to acknowledge our own tendencies and make a deliberate effort to counter these with openness and challenge our own thinking.

In summary, assertive communication is a learned behavior that requires some practice and certainly conscious thought. We are not born with the innate ability to speak assertively. We must learn the nuances of language and employ techniques to allow us to become better communicators. Try to learn the best practices below and practice them at every opportunity, whether in the workplace or relationship interactions with others. Your skills will continually evolve and improve the more you do it. Even the best communicators can improve!

Follow these assertive communication best practices:

✓ Use direct language.

✓ Start with clear observations.

✓ KISS: keep it short and simple.

✓ Ask for what you want slowly and specifically.

✓ Slow down the pace and take time to think.

✓ Avoid accusations and verbal attacks.

✓ Avoid interpretation.

✓ Clarify.

✓ Stick to the topic.

✓ Keep a "parking lot" of topics to return to.

✓ Allow the option for others to save face or rectify the situation.

Assertive Communication Exercise

Assertive communication and expressing our needs gets easier with practice. One good way to practice this is when you contact a company's customer service for a problem you are having with the product. Next time you have an issue with a company, try using the scenario below as a guide for your conversation.

Problem: After being away on vacation and having my mail held, I came back to find an overdue bill with a hefty late fee applied since the payment was not received by the due date.

Resolution: Call the credit card company's customer service line and ask them to waive the late fee.

How might the conversation go?

Initial statements:

Hello. I am a long-time customer, and this is one of my favorite credit cards. I have historically paid my balance in full and on time.

Share some facts:

I was on vacation. My mail was held. When I returned, I saw my statement and it showed a thirty-dollar late fee on a seventeen-dollar balance.

Make the request:

I am calling to see if you could please waive the late fee.

In the above scenario, the problem and request are stated simply and briefly. Facts are shared. Observations are clear. The possibility of waiving the fee leaves options for the customer service representative to rectify the situation or explore options in a nonconfrontational way. The speaker took ownership of the fact that they did not pay the bill on time. No blame was placed (despite the exorbitant fee!).

PART TWO
YOU DON'T SAY:
EMPATHIC LISTENING AND
NONVERBAL COMMUNICATION

CHAPTER 6
It Takes Energy to Engage with Empathy

Spoken communication is perhaps a contradiction in terms. Communication involves both speaking *and* listening, a bidirectional exchange, not one-way delivery. Reporting or giving a presentation is an entirely different skill, reflecting a unilateral flow of information from one to another. More commonly, in a career and throughout life, speaking is only part of the equation in connected communications. It gets most of the credit despite its limited role. When not speaking, a great communicator is an active, empathic listener who uses silence and nonverbal behaviors to enhance understanding and reinforce what is said. Effective communication involves the idea of an exchange, an interaction between two or more people, a give *and* take. How easily this is forgotten at work, in relationships, and in everyday living! The act of listening and being open to communication has far reaching implications for connecting with others, and recent studies confirm both physiological and psychological consequences of listening and nonverbal behavior in both the speaker and listener.

Counselors and other helping professionals are known for their hallmark empathic listening skills, and corporate America has touted emotional intelligence as a prerequisite for executives and business leaders. Professionals use specific techniques, often informed by research, for listening and engaging in communications that enhance understanding, build connections with others, and promote problem resolution. Anyone can learn these behaviors for better listening in everyday life and work.

What makes a good listener? Sitting silently while someone is speaking is not enough to foster understanding, and it does not convey empathy to the speaker. Looking back at elementary school, most of us were taught to sit quietly and pay attention to the teacher. This approach may be useful in learning situations but does not go far in building a connection with the one speaking. In adult life, listening solely to learn is important in some work situations and while taking a course or in a training session. More often, however, our work and adult relationships involve communications that are more bidirectional, involving one other person or a few others, and occur for the very reason of building understanding and connection. Problem-solving—a critical component in a workplace—*requires* understanding. *Empathic* listening is a way to better understand and appreciate what others say, building a connection between speaker and listener. Its importance in validating and respecting the speaker is in the facilitation of a meaningful exchange. Best practice techniques for listeners to actively engage include the following: being fully present, avoiding interruptions, using pauses effectively, passing no judgment, showing interest, taking time to absorb what is said, and surprisingly, being silent. In this chapter, we explore these behaviors and effective ways to summarize what was said and reflect for clarity, benefiting both speaker and listener. Empathy applied in a communication situation is an active, participatory behavior that facilitates understanding of another's message and the feeling behind it.

Two officemates, Lisa and Marilyn, presented a problem situation to their manager, Nancy. Marilyn was overweight and followed a strict diet. Lisa kept a candy dish on her desk, which Marilyn walked by each time she left or approached her desk. Marilyn asked Nancy to have Lisa remove the candy dish. Lisa insisted she had a right to keep what she wanted on her desk. Marilyn, you see, had a poor history of dieting and could not resist the temptation of seeing the candy dozens of times each day. She felt Lisa was sabotaging her attempts to lose weight. Lisa liked keeping candy on her desk as it invited coworkers to stop by for brief chats while they helped themselves to a treat, and because her work was solitary, Lisa sought ways to interact with others. Without empathy, neither could understand the plight of the other. Nancy simply arranged for them to move offices so as to avoid the conflict.

What if instead of quickly shuffling desks, the manager had encouraged the two employees to discuss the situation with empathy? Nancy might have guided them with tips on how to come to an understanding. Perhaps they could have set aside a time to talk privately without interruption. Allowing each a turn to explain their side to each other, giving an opportunity for them to ask each other questions, clarify needs, and better understand their differences, may have resulted in a better outcome. Had each worked to maintain a problem-solving focus, the inevitable hard feelings and animosity may have been averted. A conscious, deliberate effort to come to an understanding may have enabled each of the women to find a greater respect and empathy for each other, resulting in a more satisfying work environment for all involved. Each could maintain their self-esteem and feel validated knowing they were heard and understood. A solution need not be mutually exclusive leaving only one party satisfied. Empathic listening results in both parties feeling respected, heard, and understood. Even if a resolution is not achieved or an agreement is not reached, the respect for each party is intact and both leave with a better understanding of—and connection with—the other.

Up to this point, you've read mostly about what you can do as a speaker to improve interactions through the use of assertive communication techniques. But of course, every conversation involves people in the roles of both message sender and receiver, so what is it exactly that makes a good listener?

> **Empathy: em-pa-thy [EM-pa-thee]**
> To understand; the ability to identify with and understand somebody else's feelings or difficulties

When we listen with empathy, we are actively listening, engaging in a communication such that we are listening for understanding, not simply hearing what is being said. Not only is understanding the words and information important, successful listening also involves understanding how the speaker *feels* about what they're communicating. It is not a passive activity; it requires work. We need to intentionally engage and be ready for active participation. This is called active or empathic listening.

As listeners, if we are unable to give the speaker our full attention, it is our responsibility to make that known. We can ask for a minute to get ourselves to that point, or we can request that the discussion be postponed or rescheduled for a time when we can give it our full attention. So essential is the readiness to listen that we as speakers often take for granted and assume that our listener is ready to hear us. An unannounced important discussion often goes awry because we catch the listener at a suboptimal time in which they are unable to fully engage.

Think of a situation in which a parent arrives home from work after a harried commute, only to be welcomed at the door by an exuberant teenager bursting with a request to borrow the car for an impromptu road trip tonight. Standing there, coat still on, bag in hand, thoughts still back at the accident just witnessed on the interstate, Dad is not in the best frame of mind to hand over the keys. A recommended course of action would be for Dad to tell anxious junior something like "Give me a minute to get settled, and we can talk about it."

Presence, Engagement, and Focus

Being present for the conversation is critical. Your presence is more than just physically being there. It involves engagement and focus, perhaps even a bit of restraint. If we are caught off guard, we may react harshly or dismissively, squelching further discussion and causing offense or appearing condescending. If now is not a good time, be sure to tell the speaker that, and offer a specific time when you can give them your full attention. In the case of Marilyn and Lisa, Marilyn had confronted Lisa about the candy dish after a busy workday when Lisa was on her way out. Clearly, Lisa was not in the best position to fully engage in an awkward problem-solving conversation. Marilyn could have asked Lisa for a good time for them to talk.

Bringing ourselves right into the moment, not into the past

or future, allows us to be fully present as listeners. Our physical body posture embodies who we become; if you hold the posture of one who is completely attentive and listening, you will become a great listener. Conversely, if you are preoccupied and closed up, you conduct yourself in a manner that tells the speaker you are not fully there. The ability for our body to change our mind has been written about extensively by Harvard Business School professor Amy Cuddy and will be discussed more fully in the next chapter.[15] Lead with an open body, and open ears and mind will follow.

If you are the speaker and your listener does not seem engaged, you can also use assertive communications to help the listener engage:

- ✓ Would you please silence your phone while we talk?

- ✓ Do you mind if we sit down and talk about this privately?

- ✓ I'm having trouble talking over [the noise in the hallway, the music, etc.]?

- ✓ Can we talk quietly somewhere?

- ✓ Do you mind if I [close the door, turn down the sound, turn off the television, etc.]?

As the listener, you can also employ assertive communication to facilitate a more meaningful exchange. If approached off guard, you could respond respectfully and more effectively with "I'm preoccupied right now. Can we discuss this after lunch?" This tells the speaker you are interested in hearing them but are simply unable to give full attention right now. It also provides a specific time of when you can talk, rather than just postponing a conversation indefinitely, and expresses your sincere interest in making the most of the conversation.

When the exchange does occur and you are ready to engage, there are specific behaviors you can use that further convey interest and facilitate empathy.

Engage and Focus Fully on the Speaker

Intend to focus with all of your senses. If you are daydreaming, have your back to the speaker, are looking at your computer screen, checking your phone, or maybe even doodling, you're not giving them your full attention. The eyes are paramount here. Look directly at the speaker. Envision a cocoon with just you and the speaker, and virtually shut out the rest of the world. Keep your body facing the person—don't walk away, putter around the office, or turn your back. Avoid or eliminate any possible distractions, and don't allow anything else to invade the cocoon. If you do face an impending distraction, such as awaiting a call from the daycare center or your boss, say so and give the speaker the option to postpone the conversation. Just as a photographer fine-tunes his photo by adjusting the lens, a listener can refine their focus with small tweaks of behavior that have great impact.

In today's world, our phones are perhaps the biggest source of interruptions. It is best to silence the phone during important conversations, or even better, put the phone away. Even on vibrate mode, the buzzing of a silenced ringer distracts people. Enter the conversation with a real intent to connect. Put yourself in the best possible position to actively and fully engage with the speaker. A speaker will notice an engaged listener. An engaged listener also notices the speaker. Notice their facial expression, body language, and posture. Try to take in all possible details of the encounter.

Perhaps most important of all, train yourself to actually listen. Many times, we appear to be listening but are really just thinking about what we are going to say next. Our brains are not wired to do two things at once. We cannot simultaneously listen and think about our response at the same time. If we try to do this, much of the message is lost during this time, and this preoccupation is usually annoyingly apparent to the speaker. You will have lost the engagement and focus that active listening requires. Instead, take the time to listen, and if necessary, take a few moments after the speaker has stopped to formulate your response. It is a myth that our brains can multitask when it comes to thinking. The illusion of multitasking hides what really goes on—a rapid succession of our brain switching back and forth, inevitably with degradation of both thoughts and tasks as a result.

In coaching, the initial sessions with a client involve probing questions. People tend to quickly respond with an almost automatic response to accommodate and comply. However, real insight comes when coaches encourage clients to take a moment and *think* about the question before responding, allowing time for them to clearly formulate their thoughts or simply articulate their ambiguity. This takes practice. Slowing down the pace of listening is a skill to be learned and practiced. At first it may seem uncomfortable to pause or get in the habit of saying, "Let me think about this," before hurrying to a response. In our eagerness to engage, we often fall back on pat answers, defensive statements, or conditioned responses. Lisa, in taking time to pause and listen to Marilyn's difficulty with food triggers, would have gained an understanding of how hard Marilyn has been trying to lose weight in an attempt to lower her blood pressure. As a single mother, Marilyn is concerned that her poor health could keep her from being the best mom she can be. Lisa, it turns out, lives alone and felt very isolated. Her interactions with coworkers are the highlight of her day. The candy is a means for Lisa to draw others to her desk and connect. Neither knew these facts about the other. As engaged listeners, they could discover new perspectives to help them see the problem as small compared to the bigger struggles each experiences outside of work. Only through thoughtful, unhurried exchanges can we truly share insightful, meaningful information. In normal conversations, try using the under-utilized tool of the pause, and notice how well it allows a conversation to quickly uncover meaning and foster connection. Slow down the pace and start connecting. Not only will you listen better, but you may also discover clarity in your own thoughts.

Avoid Interrupting

Human brains have an innate impulsivity that can derail even the best intentions to listen carefully. This impulsivity is a carryover from our primitive brains, and though less adaptive in modern times, it was once adaptive for survival in harsh physical environments. Vigilance against threats in the physical environment and the ability to react quickly was critical for remaining alive in early human evolution. Fortunately, most conversations today do not occur in such conditions, but our evolved yet still impulsive brains must be reined in a bit to refrain from interrupting when someone is speaking.

You may recall a few years ago when, during a music awards show, Kanye West interrupted Taylor Swift's acceptance of an award. Viewers the world over were dismayed by this clear breach of decorum. With this interruption, as in all interruptions, Kanye showed Taylor and the world he thought what he had to say was more important than what she was saying. Not only is this interruption—and indeed all of them—rude; it robs the speaker of validation. It conveys to the speaker that they don't matter and, in doing so, prohibits understanding. In everyday conversations, the tendency to interrupt is often great as our brains are predisposed to impulsivity, but the following techniques can be used to tame that inner tiger clamoring to be heard:

- ✓ Let the speaker finish talking.

- ✓ Jot down a quick note of your thoughts to share when they finish.

- ✓ Quickly return your attention to the speaker.

- ✓ Come back to your thoughts when they finish.

- ✓ Use a pause to gather your thoughts when it is time to respond.

You can't concentrate on what someone is saying if you are busy formulating what you're going to say next. And the speaker may read your facial expressions and sense that you aren't really listening, causing a loss in your credibility as an engaged listener. By waiting to compose your responses until after the speaker ends their statement, you gain more information and allow yourself time to prepare a better response. Listening is not the same as waiting for your turn to talk. Rather than a badminton match, communication is more akin to dancing with a partner.

One-upmanship also has no place in good communication. An example of this would be "If you think that's bad, you should hear what happened to me." Many of us have experienced that friend or coworker who, in an effort to show solidarity, agrees with our plight and rushes on to say they know how it feels because it happened to them. Then they continue on and detail their experience, which may or may not be at all like yours. They have commandeered the conversation. In an effort to show support, they have undermined their listening and your message, and true connection is lost.

Empathy does not require having experienced the same thing; supportive, empathic listening requires respect for the uniqueness of the individual's experiences and truly hearing what is being said. It doesn't even require you to have a solution; your presence, focus, and interest is often enough. Redirecting a conversation to your concerns not only exemplifies poor taste, it shows the speaker that you value their expressed thoughts less than your own, and it minimizes real connection and understanding. It thwarts further discussion. It is not empathic listening.

Don't Judge, Show Interest

To effectively communicate with someone, it is not necessary to agree with what is being said. It is possible to listen empathically to understand and yet not like what you hear. You may not like the speaker or their values or opinions, but you *can* listen without blame, criticism, and judgment. Sometimes, even the most difficult communication can lead to insight and could result in a surprisingly pleasant exchange. Be open to that possibility. Going in with preconceived notions of how things might go and putting up defenses as you hear what is said will detract from true understanding and empathy.

A speaker appreciates when the listener shows interest in what they are saying. You don't have to clap, but a smile goes a long way. A bit of encouragement with an occasional nod is helpful. It is good to show some emotion and avoid the stone-faced expression. Some positive response (action) from the listener keeps the speaker on track to articulate their thoughts. Keep your posture open and inviting (see chapter 7). And encourage the speaker to continue with a brief acknowledgment—a simple "yes" or "uh-huh" is sufficient. These listening behaviors build positivity in both speaker and listener and foster connection between them.

Mirror, Mirror

Rephrasing is another critical part of empathic listening. It demonstrates that you listened and understood what is being said. To do this, you can use similar wording to mirror back what the speaker said to confirm their intended meaning. Sometimes after hearing the listener's paraphrasing, the speaker will correct or clarify. Reflecting back gives the speaker a chance to refine their message so you as listener can better understand. If the message is long, you can summarize the main points. It is best to use the speaker's words, however, rather than to substitute your words, which may reveal subtle differences in meaning. Avoid any assumptions.

For example, if the speaker said he was angry, don't rephrase this as *furious* because the substituted word doesn't accurately reflect the stated intensity. It is important to acknowledge any stated emotion. When that emotion is anger, an acknowledgment helps to diffuse the anger and steer the conversation toward resolution. Only restate emotion when in fact it was stated; don't assume you know how the other feels. Be careful not to interpret an emotion, for example, don't assume anger when a speaker shares frustration—these are different emotions and only the speaker can interpret their own emotions. Questioning is also part of rephrasing. If you are unclear about something, ask the speaker to clarify by asking questions like "How do you mean?" "Tell me more about that," or "Help me understand." Asking questions is a great way to show interest in what is being said because it forces elaboration. To accept statements without asking any questions leaves the speaker wondering if you actually heard them, got their meaning, or perhaps tuned them out entirely.

The pause is perhaps the single most underutilized tool of effective listening. Pausing after the speaker has finished allows you time to process what was said. Those few moments give the brain a chance to take it in, mull it over a bit, and make sense of it. Then you can reflect what was said back to the speaker, paraphrase, and distill it down to the major points, allowing the speaker to hear what they said in a new way and maybe further clarify or even modify if they were ambiguous. Paraphrasing also helps the speaker to look more objectively at their idea, and they may retract an extreme statement or soften the message when they hear it repeated back to them. It's like singing karaoke. You think you're the next American Idol until you watch that video your friend made, and you hear yourself. The playback helps you discover things you might want to change or refine in your next rendition.

We can all become better listeners. In doing so, we fully support the speaker to create a safe, welcoming space in which thoughts can easily flow and be understood. Practicing the behaviors of empathic, active listeners will improve our skills and ultimately enhance our connections with others.

In summary, empathic listening requires specific behaviors that facilitate understanding. A good listener establishes an empathic presence that signals their readiness to engage. They minimize interruptions or notify the speaker if an interruption is expected due to known factors. They show interest and rephrase content to clarify what was said. A good listener is nonjudgmental despite any difference in opinion. These behaviors are sometimes challenging and require practice, but the effort will be worth it.

CHAPTER 7
Is Your Body Working for You or against You?

I n communications, body language—including movements of the head, eyes, face, posture, and gestures—is a big contributor to the spoken message. It can either reinforce or contradict spoken words. We can learn to be fluent in our own body language and use it to support and strengthen our message. While listening and speaking, our bodies also play a crucial role in how we are perceived despite how credible our content is. It is important to match our body language to our words, thereby managing others' perceptions of our intent and credibility. The style of body language we use in listening and speaking must also be appropriate for the situation, whether greeting a foreign dignitary or a group of old friends, otherwise things may not go as planned. Respect for personal space and sensitivity to cultural norms requires us to adapt our body language with agility. This chapter includes an exercise in interpreting body language and its impact on the perceived message, underscoring the need for body language to be precise and specific.

Why Is Body Language Important?

Now for the fun stuff about communicating: nonverbal communications and body language. Often overlooked, we will see that body language in fact plays a big part in the message we give *and* get. Body language involves more than just facial expressions. The movement of our head, where the eyes are focused and how they move, our posture, how we are standing or sitting, and our hand gestures all contribute to the message we give and receive. Head, eyes, face, posture, and gestures together compose body language and influence message delivery and receipt.

Whenever we are in a situation in which there are people listening to a speaker, we can observe body language and its influence on our perceptions. We can think about what listeners might be saying with their body language, and ask ourselves these questions:

✓ Are they open to what is being said?

✓ Do they seem interested in the speaker?

✓ Are they relaxed or uptight?

✓ Are they preoccupied or distracted?

✓ Are they guarded or inviting?

Although each of us could identify different interpretations of the same scene, as perceivers of body language, we may discern something other than the intended message. Listeners may be unaware of their posture or expressions. When I share photos of workplace groups in workshops, each participant writes down their interpretation of what is happening in each photo. We collect them and read them aloud. Aside from garnering a few laughs, the exercise highlights the variability in possible interpretations of the same behavior. In truth, we don't really know what is meant without situational cues and a deeper understanding of how nonverbal behaviors influence communication. It is clear, however, that nonverbal behavior does influence *our perceptions*, regardless of its accuracy.

As readers, you can do a similar exercise as follows. Look at the people in figure 7.1. Write down what immediately comes to mind about the exhibited behavior and its message. What are these people saying with their body language?

Figure 7.1: Body language vignettes

Myriad interpretations exist for the behaviors depicted in figure 7.1. Because the intentions are ambiguous, a perceiver may consider various possibilities:

1. Is this woman daydreaming? Watching the clock? Is the speaker entering from a side door?

2. Is this man praying that the meeting ends soon? Is he upset about what he's hearing, perhaps? Is he bracing himself for a layoff?

3. Is this employee near the edge, literally pulling her hair out?

4. Does this man's clasped hands mean he is not receptive to the new idea or simply anxious?

5. Is this man thinking about the argument he had with his girlfriend last night, daydreaming about the weekend plans, or seriously contemplating the solution you just presented?

6. Is this man giving mixed messages? Though he is looking directly at me, the hands in pockets might indicate something is being withheld.

7. Will this woman burst forth from the desk and exert physical force? Is she confronting someone, or just exhausted and holding herself up? This forceful pose could be perceived as intimidating, particularly if others are seated.

8. Will this woman collapse if you put just one more paper on her desk? Is she overwhelmed or dreading what I have to say? Or, is she simply tired, having just finished a difficult project?

While these possible interpretations may or may not make sense, without situational context and spoken words, we can't be sure what is intended. We don't really know what listeners are saying with their body language. What we do know is that nonverbal cues influence *our perceptions* of whether or not they are listening to what we say. Our brains want to attribute reasons for behavior. We make interpretations, albeit erroneous, on why people act. If we are speaking and those listening exhibit confusing body language, we try to decipher it. They may be completely unaware of their body language and our perceptions.

Conversely, if we as speakers exhibit body language that is ambiguous, contradicts our words, or is offensive, our message can be distorted or diminished because of its inconsistency with our actions. The very same body language may be acceptable in one situation and not another. We may interpret it based on the wrong context. A pat on the back with words of encouragement may be warmly regarded among players during a sporting match but is considered harassment in an office setting.

How can we better utilize and understand body language to enhance our message and listening ability? Awareness is the first step in developing nonverbal communications skills. By being aware of the ambiguity of cues given by body language alone, we can start to become conscious of our own body language and position ourselves to be perceived in the way we want to be perceived.

Our body should not conflict with our words. Our body should enhance a conversation, not inhibit it. We can use our bodies to improve our messages *and* our listening. Nonverbal signals should match up with the words. Nonverbal communication should reinforce what is being said, not contradict it. If you say one thing but your body language says something else, your listener is likely to feel you're being dishonest or may become confused. For example, don't say yes while shaking your head no.

We've all seen politicians pounding the podium to underscore their message. Many use gestures, stances, and full body movements to emphasize a point and convey confidence and power. When professionals give a speech, their body language has often been coached to ensure it reinforces their message and elicits a particular response from the audience—such as garnering their support, vote, or donation, rallying for a cause or inciting rage at injustice. These situations are calculated and rehearsed, much more so than our everyday conversations and exchanges with others. Adapting body language to fit the situation and the listener is crucial to getting it right in various settings. For example, that same politician may use different body language with a diplomat than they would with a child. They may use a more formal pose with the dignitaries, squat down low to meet a child's gaze, and use more gestures and facial expressions with friends. You, too, as a person who communicates in many different situations, must adapt your style to the context and be aware of your listener and the situation to determine what body language is appropriate.

In everyday communication, our body language should be more authentic. When it matches our message, we better communicate our thoughts and feelings. When we are listening and aware of our body language, we can encourage a speaker and elicit true connection.

Use these techniques for better body language:

✓ Use open posture.

- Uncross your arms.

- Stand with an open stance.

- Sit leaning forward.

- Maintain eye contact.

- Face the speaker.

✓ Enhance your verbal message with your body.

✓ Keep consistency between body and words.

✓ Adjust your body language to the context.

As with all skills we develop, awareness of our current behavior and go-to style is a springboard for positive change. Once we begin to take notice of our bodies and movements and become aware of how we present ourselves and how others present themselves, we can assess how well a presentation matches the spoken dialogue. We can also account for individual differences. Thinking about someone's age, culture, religion, gender, and emotional states when reading body language signals helps us interpret meaning or identify questions when the meaning is unclear. An American teenager and an Asian business-man, for example, are likely to use nonverbal signals and inflection differently because of each group's cultural norms and stages of life.

But those cues alone don't complete the whole picture. Look at nonverbal communication signals as a group. Don't read too much into a single gesture or nonverbal cue. Consider all the nonver-bal signals you receive—from eye contact to tone of voice to body language—as a total message. Anyone can slip up occasionally and fail to maintain eye contact, for example, or briefly cross their arms inadvertently. To avoid misinterpretation of a single cue, look at the signals as a whole to get a better read on a person's message. But be careful not to make assumptions. If cues are ambiguous or contradictory, that is a perfect opportunity to ask for clarification. You could say, "You are nodding in agreement, yet you seem to be frowning," or "Can you help me understand what you think?" This type of response allows you to share your interpretation of their reaction and ask for clarity in a nonthreatening manner. Another way to facilitate connection is to use body language to convey positive feelings. An occasional nod or smile shows positive encouragement. It is difficult to feel connected when we feel threatened or negativity coming our way. If we learn to use our body to enhance our message, invite understanding and exude positive encouragement, it becomes an asset in our pursuit of becoming a better communicator.

To improve nonverbal communication, try the following techniques:

- ✓ Practice observing others.

- ✓ Respect individual differences (age, gender, culture, religion, emotional state, etc.).

- ✓ Consider nonverbal signals as a whole.

- ✓ Convey positive feelings with body language.

Body Language Exercise

Connecting through nonverbal communication involves so many factors. Though most of us will not need the formal coaching a political candidate would employ, anyone can learn to better use nonverbal behaviors to facilitate more positive, engaging communication. This exercise will get you started on the path to improve your nonverbal communication.

1. Practice observing people communicating in public places such as in a restaurant, at the mall, or while waiting for a bus. Select a particular conversation to study,

and jot down your thoughts on each of the following to develop your awareness of nonverbal communications in others:

    a. Who are they?

    b. Notice how they react to each other.

    c. What might they be talking about?

    d. What is their relationship?

2. For the situation you are observing, think about the factors that dictate appropriate body language—age, gender, culture, emotional state, and other situational cues. Write down your observations for each of the following:

    a. Are the speakers and listeners using body language appropriate to each of these factors?

    b. Note any discrepant behaviors or inconsistent cues. What could they do differently to remove the contradictions?

3. Repeat this for several other situations of various contexts and participants.

4. What have you learned from observing others' body language and nonverbal cues?

5. Were there any behaviors you noticed in others that you also exhibit yourself on occasion?

    a. Which of these are helpful in keeping your body language and nonverbal behavior consistent with your intended message?

    b. Which behaviors seem to hinder consistency with the message?

    c. Which serve to foster connection with the other person?

    d. For any that hinder connection, what could be done instead, or what behavior could be employed to better foster a connection?

By observing others, you also become more aware of yourself and others' nonverbal signals when communicating. Being aware of current behaviors gives us a benchmark from which to move toward more effective and positive levels of connection. By knowing our current state, we can compare it with our desired future state of empathy, giving us a target behavior for which to strive. Awareness is the springboard for change.

CHAPTER 8
The Brain as a Listening Organ

Typically, people think the main body parts involved in communication are the ears and mouth. The brain, however, has the starring role, both directing and acting in the communications movie. Psychologists have long studied the attitude-behavior connection, examining which one influences and which one is influenced, like the age-old question of which comes first—the chicken or the egg. Groundbreaking research on the physiological changes that occur based on our body language and attitudes tells us that not only others' perceptions but also our perception of ourselves changes as a result of our behavior. The brain is both influenced by what we do and also influences what we do! Our feelings, attitudes, and self-perceptions are not all in our head—the body plays an enormous and guiding role. Several unexpected findings reveal behaviors that mold our views of ourselves and others. Our recollection of events is distorted depending on intensity and duration, and we can consider these factors in devising our communications. We can practice techniques informed by science to empower us in difficult conversations, minimize stress, and mitigate the ever-present biases that exist in the brain.

Body language affects not only how others see us, it also changes how we see ourselves.

Our Behavior Drives Our Attitude

Social psychologists spend enormous amounts of research dollars and time studying nonverbal communications. People draw conclusions when viewing nonverbal communications in others. Sweeping judgments are made based on body language. Others judge us based on body cues—right or wrong. While this idea is nothing new, what is new is the recent research that we are influenced by *our own* nonverbal expressions. Our thoughts, attitudes, and confidence are driven by what we are doing with our body at any given moment, as shown in figure 8.1.

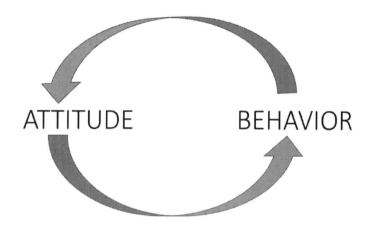

Figure 8.1: Attitude behavior influence cycle

To get a better understanding of this discreet influencer, think about how you are sitting right now: Are your arms crossed or legs folded? Are you leaning in?

Take note of what you are doing and become aware of the body language you are using, perhaps noticing for the first time your go-to position. What could this position be telling others about you, and what is it telling you about yourself? Is it the image you intend to portray? Are you sending an unintended message?

The body's behavior sends messages to our brain, and our brain sends messages to our body. Our attitude is not always a deliberate entity that directs our behavior; sometimes it results from messages our body sends to our brain, thereby directed *by* our behavior.

Empowering Posture

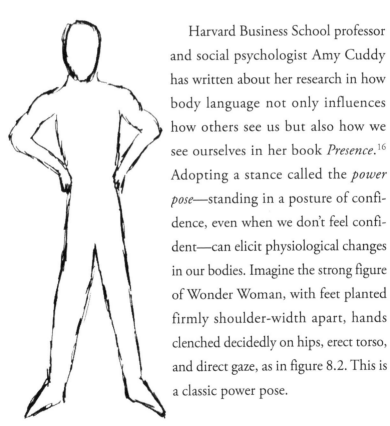

Harvard Business School professor and social psychologist Amy Cuddy has written about her research in how body language not only influences how others see us but also how we see ourselves in her book *Presence*.[16] Adopting a stance called the *power pose*—standing in a posture of confidence, even when we don't feel confident—can elicit physiological changes in our bodies. Imagine the strong figure of Wonder Woman, with feet planted firmly shoulder-width apart, hands clenched decidedly on hips, erect torso, and direct gaze, as in figure 8.2. This is a classic power pose.

Figure 8.2: Power pose

Cuddy's research calls to mind the behavior of animals in the wild. In nature, expressions of power and dominance are adaptive for animals, where the survival instinct takes precedence. Imagine gorillas beating their chest, lions adopting an expansive stance when they roar, and grizzly bears waving arms ferociously at their prey. These are all expressions of dominance. Establishing presence is an adaptive behavior for animals faced with a threat or predator, as explained in Charles Darwin's theory of survival of the fittest. Humans too can express dominance and power by making ourselves bigger by extending our limbs, maintaining erect posture, and taking up more space. Though our brains have evolved, humans are still driven by laws of nature and survival instincts.

The power pose has been shown to alter hormonal levels of testosterone (associated with dominance) and cortisol (associated with stress). Elevated levels of testosterone and lowered cortisol levels can positively impact our chances for success. Cuddy's research shows that spending only two minutes in a power pose can trigger hormonal changes in the brain. Try doing the power pose for two minutes (in private) just before any stressful interaction—a job interview, difficult meeting, or asking for a raise. By doing so, you are reconfiguring your brain to better position yourself for the situation.

Adopting the power pose involves a few simple thoughts and actions:

✓ Make yourself big, like animals in the wild.

✓ Stand with feet planted shoulder-width apart.

✓ Take up space and establish your presence.

✓ Rest your fists on your hips. Feel your rib cage expand.

✓ Think, "Survival of the fittest!"

✓ Take slow, deep belly breaths.

✓ Remain like this for two minutes.

If you are nervous about an upcoming event, like an important presentation or a first date, for example, you can use positive body language to signal confidence, even though you may not be feeling it. Instead of tentatively entering a room with your head down, eyes averted, and sliding into a chair, try standing tall with your shoulders back, smiling, maintaining eye contact, and delivering a firm handshake. It will make you feel more self-confident and also helps put other people at ease. When we pretend to be powerful, we also start to feel more powerful. Similarly, when we force ourselves to smile, we can also begin to feel more positive. We are profoundly influenced by our own actions. Our attitudes not only cause us to act in certain ways, they are directly affected by our behavior.

Another interesting finding in Cuddy's work is our tendency, in power situations, to use opposite nonverbal and body language than that of the person we are with. If they are powerful, we withdraw. If they are loud, we talk softly. This can be maladaptive, especially if we are facing a dominant, aggressive person. In these situations, we do not tend to mirror body language—rather, we use opposite body language. While the evidence shows we are influenced by our own actions, we must use our actions to our advantage. If we act submissive or passive, it can be physically or socially dangerous. The opposite behavior tendency is disadvantageous. Awareness of it allows us to then choose a more appropriate action. For example, we can meet aggression with confidence and by standing our ground.

Sheryl Sandberg, in her book *Lean In,* also talks about the importance of physical presence and leaning right in at the boardroom table.[17] Establishing your presence also works in the lunchroom or staff meeting. Sandberg advises "Fake it till you make it," indicating that even if you are not feeling comfortable or confident in a situation, acting so enables feelings to change so that you do feel more confident and comfortable. She contends you aren't faking it; you *are* it. Cuddy goes even further, stating, "Fake it till you become it," showing physiologically how our brains change and *become* it. Adopting the behavior alters our attitudes and feelings. Act powerful, and you will feel more powerful. Even less-stressful situations can be improved with the power pose. One of my executive clients found that he felt more decisive and confident in conversations while standing in the power pose during phone calls than while seated at his desk. If you work in an office, taking an opportunity to stand during calls gives the added physical benefit of standing in addition to the psychological confidence boost.

Ganesh is an account executive for a media agency. His daily workday involves phone calls, video calls, and in-person meetings with clients and the ad team. His easygoing nature suits his role well, and he is mainly unflappable when it comes to solving clients' problems. One client, however, posed a particular challenge for Ganesh because of her demanding, aggressive style and tendency to complain. Ganesh winced whenever calls from that client came in and felt his usual confidence waning. Ganesh realized that he felt less confident with this client, although his competency and ability to solve her issues was undeniable. He began to practice "faking it" whenever her calls came in. He had posted a reminder on his computer screensaver that ushered in bold letters across the screen saying "Fake it!" in an effort to recall the idea of acting in the way he wished to project. When those calls came in, he adopted a position of confidence even though he didn't initially feel confident. He also began using the power pose. Upon taking this client's calls, he immediately asked her to hold a minute while he got up from his desk and assumed the power pose. Upon resuming the call, Ganesh had the presence to engage more confidently and started to feel more competent after only a few calls. His actions guided his thoughts to enable him to think and feel more confident.

The Power of Role Play

The idea that our behavior influences our attitudes has far-reaching implications for coaching and personal development. It underscores the importance of role-playing and practice for interactions that we expect to be difficult. If we pretend we are confident, capable, and powerful, then we can become it. Pretending has been shown to be effective for children in learning new roles, mastering their environment, and establishing ways of behaving in various situations. While children naturally pretend, as adults, we seem to have lost that power of acting or pretending. We typically don't role-play or pretend when we have to learn something new. But why not? The research serves as a reminder that we must resurrect those old tools of childhood and try out behaviors we want to adopt and internalize.

Role-playing is a tool often used by coaches to encourage clients to try out various approaches for interacting with others. It allows the client to become more comfortable and confident in a behavior in a safe environment. And role-playing can be practiced without a coach. You can role-play using a smartphone to record yourself, speaking as yourself and also voicing anticipated responses from the other party. Or make a video of yourself, taking the opportunity to observe your body language as well as verbal response. Repeating this and replaying it can solidify a desired communication or behavior so that when the time comes you are ready. Another way to role-play is to enlist the help of a friend to act as the other party in the anticipated scenario, better preparing you for the upcoming challenge.

The implications of increased confidence and power are significant in common career experiences like job interviews, performance reviews, sales meetings, and presentations. Your credibility as a speaker has more to do with your behavior than your content and knowledge. Cuddy has also shown that the level of confidence you have while giving a speech increases listeners' rating of speech content, even if that content is poor! Some politicians have mastered this concept. By displaying powerful, confident behavior, they establish connections with their supporters, often despite their message.

So, we have seen how extraordinarily complex communication really is, involving not only what we say and how we listen but also what our bodies do. For communications, body language is so much more than nonverbal cues. It often provides the missing puzzle piece that allows the full meaning of an encounter to emerge.

Consider this: Our actions influence our thoughts, our thoughts influence our actions, and what we do changes what happens

Barriers

In home renovations, breaking down walls is gratifying. It is a means of opening up the space, expanding the view, pushing past obstacles, and removing barriers. It is often exhilarating. Like an old home, our communications can be improved with removal of unnecessary barriers that can sabotage good communications. So often we shut down communications before they even get started. Another person, either intentionally or inadvertently, may shut us down through their actions, words, or how they express themselves.

Whether we are the speaker or listener, both roles present challenges. Through awareness, we can begin to minimize the common barriers to effective communication:

- ✗ lack of awareness

- ✗ filters

- ✗ language inhibitors

- ✗ poison words

- ✗ bias

- ✗ style/schema

- ✗ timing

- ✗ negativity

- ✗ passivity/aggression

- ✗ distractions

✗ noise

✗ body language

In earlier chapters we examined these pitfalls and associated practical techniques to overcome them. In addition, several natural obstacles exist within the brain, uncovered by Daniel Kahneman in his decades of research on decision-making and cognitive bias. Interesting studies on how people value and remember various life experiences, especially negative ones, illuminate the role of memory.[18] Kahneman and Fredrickson found that no matter how bad an experience was, nor how long it lasted, people use only a few critical moments to characterize an entire experience.

The experiments involved numerous situations including medical procedures, pain studies, and simple laboratory tests with subjects submerging their hands in cold water for various lengths of time and in various temperatures. Kahneman and his team confirmed the existence of two biases, which he calls the *peak-end rule* and *duration neglect*. With duration neglect, we erroneously perceive length of time when remembering experiences. Our memory poorly captures how long or short an experience is. With peak-end rule, our ratings of an experience can be predicted by its intensity at the worst and last moments. Overall or actual intensity is not captured well in our memory. The brain remembers an experience based on its characteristics at the beginning, the peak, and the end, not as an average or sum of all moments within an experience.

In communications, these theories inform how best to mitigate recollection of long or intense interactions. We can address the peak-end rule by ending our difficult conversations on a high note despite having some unpleasant moments during the conversation, thus ensuring that everyone involved views the interaction more positively. So, when you wrap up a generally unpleasant conversation or if your exchange did not go as well as you had intended, try to end it with some positivity. Your interaction will be perceived better than it really was! Your statements, demeanor, and level of respect at the beginning and end of the conversation can influence how that conversation is remembered. Paying more attention to how we end and begin conversations leverages the peak-end rule bias to positively influence how the entire encounter is remembered.

In the workplace, a common stress-producing encounter is the employee performance appraisal. Managers and employees alike often dread these occasions. The very nature of these discussions requires a review of positive and negative work behaviors and productivity. However, informed by the peak-end rule, we can take action that facilitates remembering these occasions more positively. We can start and end these conversations on a positive note. We can temper negative feedback with congratulatory feedback and encouragement at the end of the review. We can avoid jumping right in with the bad news or punitive statements, sharing worst case examples using less intense language. We can express gratitude for participation and feedback at the beginning and end.

Because of the brain's duration neglect bias, elapsed time is not usually remembered well. Whether five minutes or twenty-five minutes, people often cannot accurately recall how long a conversation lasts. Our sense of time is marked instead by the three milestone points—the beginning, peak, and end. The peak is judged as less aversive if the intensity is diminished to a lesser intensity by the end, even if the experience is longer than a shorter experience with the same peak. It seems duration is not used to judge an aversive experience. In the performance review conversation, we could apply the duration bias by spending more time discussing positive feedback instead of delivering negative feedback in a shorter discussion. Intense negative experiences with fading intensity after peaking would be remembered more positively.

Recognizing these natural biases that exist in our brain can guide how we handle times in which we must deliver or receive bad news. Terminations, job rejections, declining job offers, and negotiations can be more positively remembered if we consider and control our actions in the beginning, peak, and end of any aversive encounter. Be sure to end on the positive, with a smile, gradually diminish peak negative feedback, and take the opportunity to say thank you before closing. Your conversation will be more positively recalled despite negative messaging within it.

PART THREE
BUSY IS THE NEW BLACK:
FASHIONABLY MANAGE YOUR TIME

CHAPTER 9
There's No Time Like the Present

Let's face it. There are not enough hours in a day to get everything done. Or *are* there? Time eludes us even though we now have technology that supposedly saves us time. No longer must we procure stamps, find an envelope, pen a letter, and mail it to get our message to a hopeful receiver days later. We have email, Facebook, and text messaging, as well as mobile phones, should we desire to make a call and (gasp!) conduct a real-time conversation with someone. So where has all this saved time gone? Why do we still feel that the time available is inadequate? The answer is when we are not looking, we let time manage us. It has become fashionable to have a calendar booked through the next seven weeks. Busy is acceptable, even expected, and obliterates many a would-be meeting or get-together. Time, when uncontrolled, takes what it will, unabashedly vying for our attention with myriad temptations that allure and sidetrack us, keeping us from getting things done. But we humans have the upper hand. We can learn to manage time and come to enjoy doing so.

A recurring theme among my clientele is the challenge of managing time, focusing on what is most important, and setting priorities. Execution of the best intentions is often elusive, with distractions and procrastination interfering incessantly. This chapter introduces the concept of values-based prioritization, a straightforward way of making choices that support our goals and values and empowering us to manage our time and focus in such a way that our values become the compass by which to navigate.

It is a gift to the self to learn to set priorities and manage our use of time. Myths exist as to why we cannot do it, and yet basic strategies and practices can defy those myths and enable readers to use choice in tackling priorities and optimizing their schedule. Whether using manual methods or technology apps, the best practices for getting ahead of the clock can be learned now.

Busy versus Balanced

Most people are already doing some time management at work or for school. Our success in doing so, however, relies on our ability to exercise deliberate choices based on our values and the implementation of best practices to support them. Often the need for better time management pops up suddenly at inopportune times—such as when we get busy or overwhelmed by the workload. In my coaching, clients cite many sources and reasons for poor time management: there are just too many demands on our time; the workload never ends; our schedules are jam-packed, and schedules change frequently on any given day of the week; and we are busy juggling work, school, family, leisure, and social engagements, all while trying to maintain our health and well-being. Busy seems the fashionable hallmark of today. Haven't we all said to friends, coworkers, and family, "I'd *love* to join you at the [fill in the blank: gym, party, restaurant, etc.], but I'm just too *busy*"? Usually followed by a deep sigh, we see our friend shaking their head and rolling their eyes. Busy is the little black dress of the excuse wardrobe. What if we refreshed our closet, tossed out *busy*, and replaced it with *balance*?

Busy families have umpteen kids' activities; busy professionals have jam-packed schedules of meetings, travel, and conference calls; small business owners are busy navigating network events between business hours; and students are busy with extracurriculars and beefing up their résumé with experiences. The pace of life has outdistanced our capacity to be involved. While some place the blame on our fascination with screen time, the real culprit is our own lack of prioritizing what is truly important to us. Setting priorities and articulating a few key values helps us keep balanced when the scale of life starts to tip to one side.

For some of us, our schedules are too packed to even think about what is important to us, yet doing so helps us realize we are spending time doing everything *but* those things. By thinking about and especially listing out what is really important to us (our top two to three values and goals), we can then use our stated priorities as a litmus test for those pesky time wasters and commitments that compete for our attention and time. That litmus test is the start of going from busy to balanced. Consider the following example.

Mai defined her values and goals list to be:

- spending time with family

- training for the half-marathon

- working extra to save for that vacation

- having a weekly lunch with girlfriends

- planting the garden

Then a friend asked Mai to start a new cooking class with her on Wednesdays. The busy Mai would impulsively accept (it does sound fun) and then scramble to make it there every week, darting from work early, leaving the kids sour, wallet lighter, and the garden full of weeds. The busy Mai would not consult her list of goals, responding quickly without considering the implications. The busy Mai had not posted that infamous list on her computer screen, calendar, bathroom mirror, and refrigerator as a constant reminder of her values to keep her on the track she set for herself.

The new balanced Mai, however, would first check the list, which acts as a continuous reminder as her screensaver, phone wallpaper, and fridge note. She sees that "developing cooking skills" is not on there. The balanced Mai would decline, saying something like "Thanks, that sounds fun if I were free. Wednesdays are my distance run days, and, in March, I am using Wednesdays to start the garden. I definitely want to hear all about it when we have lunch together though." (Notice no apologies are given.) Responding to her friend in this way has a significant impact on Mai's quest to uphold her values, focus on her priorities, and maintain her friendship in the following ways:

✓ Her friend feels validated.

✓ Her priorities (the half-marathon and garden) are maintained.

✓ She has allowed herself flexibility to work late or help with homework those nights, if needed, by not adding another activity to the schedule.

✓ She reminds her friend (and herself) that they will see each other at the weekly lunch.

✓ She realizes she has control over how to spend her time.

With this newly exercised freedom of choice and values mindset, we see that it is possible to make better choices with our time for ourselves and allow us to really live the kind of life we envision. By intentionally choosing what we do, we empower ourselves to be less busy and yet more productive in a way that brings less stress and more satisfaction and reinforces our stated values and priorities.

When we practice *intentional living,* in which we manage our time before it manages us, we can often minimize or eliminate the distractions that vie for our attention and time. Intentional living involves continuously measuring our use of time against our personal priorities and goals. The stated list becomes an invaluable tool that can measure the worthiness of any task, request, or demand competing for our time. When we ask ourselves "Is this task helping me to get further along toward my goal of _____?" and "Is this task relevant to my top priorities?" we allow ourselves a chance to evaluate whether it makes sense to spend any time on it. Each of us has our own set of priorities and values. Our schedule is unique to each of us, and it is important to recognize that we do have choices. By posting the list prominently to remind ourselves of what is important to us and the goals we want to achieve, we have a handy reminder to help us stay on track. Placing the list of basic values and priorities front and center in our world is a way to guide our choices. The list facilitates decisions and can accept blame when tough choices arise.

The objectivity of the list takes some of the heat and stress from you and offers clarity when your judgment may be clouded.

My clients have used clever ways to keep their list readily available. Sticky notes, screensavers, phone apps with periodic reminders, task lists on Outlook, Alexa, or personal assistant automated reminders—there are countless ways technology can help us stay focused on the important things lest we forget. Calling our attention to our values enables us to choose to support them, ferreting out those activities that are counter, inconsistent, or detrimental. The clarity gained from frequent references to our stated goals also holds us accountable, and follow-through becomes more likely. Frequent checks of the list can become part of our normal routine, so that as we plan our schedule for a given week, we can make adjustments as needed when our priorities change.

The list also cannot be so rigid that it prevents flexibility. If the list is too restrictive or outdated, it loses its value and thwarts any further effort to remain focused on what is truly important. I recommend reviewing the list regularly to see if any adjustments are necessary. If the list changes too frequently, that may indicate a need to refine or solidify your values and goals with specific language to gain clarity.

Thought-Action Conundrum

Awareness of our own thinking and behavior creates the benchmark against which we can begin to see change. How we think about priorities and our use of time in comparison to our actual behaviors and decisions must be considered so we can intentionally think and choose wisely for a more positive focus. Sometimes our thinking is clouded by myths, and unfortunately there are many misconceptions about managing time:

- ✗ Only disorganized people need to manage their time.

- ✗ I can remember what I need to do.

- ✗ I will become rigid or inflexible if I schedule everything.

- ✗ I cannot follow a schedule.

- ✗ There's not enough time for all I must do.

It is easy to think we just need to work more to get everything done. Early in my career, a manager once shared with me the motto "Work smarter, not harder," and it has made a lasting impression. With the philosophy of working smart, this manager set limits on the workload, thereby granting more time to get tasks done efficiently. Another leader I worked with shared his guiding principle of only taking on engagements he knew the company could deliver successfully. By not taking on risky projects or those that might require resources he didn't have, this leader selectively chose his customers to optimize his business. Each of these leaders had his or her own strategies, and you, too, will develop your own strategies for successfully managing priorities as time goes on. Learning and using some of the best practice techniques can help you create your unique strategy and guiding principles too.

Surveys show that time management is one of the most difficult things in many jobs. In some occupations, managing time is especially important due to variability of the work. When the job involves various tasks over the course of a workday or work week, how time is allocated makes a significant impact on the quality and quantity of the work product. Having multiple demands and tasks, each requiring different skills and cognitive processes, logistics alone present a challenge. The modern basics of time management can help us fit it all in:

- ✓ Choose wisely (intentional living).

- ✓ Establish priorities and work on them.

- ✓ Measure any possible tasks against your true values and goals.

- ✓ Create routine among chaos.

- ✓ Exercise discipline and practice making informed choices.

- ✓ Pick a technology method and start using it exclusively.

The fundamental concept of managing time and using values-based prioritization is that there are choices to be made. We simply cannot do everything that comes up. We have limited time and energy. Some things are simply not worth our time. We can easily get distracted from our true north and commit to doing things we don't want or need to do as time marches on.

Consider the following hypothetical example in figure 9.1:

Figure 9.1: Breakdown of a given work week

168 hours in a seven-day week
- 56 hours sleeping
- 40 hours working
- 10 hours eating (~1.5 hours daily)
- 10 hours commuting
= 52 hours left per week for everything else

52 hours a week equates to ~7.5 hours daily for family, health and fitness, social, personal activities, and leisure time.

The work week breakdown in figure 9.1 illustrates how limited our time really is. Of course, your week may break down differently depending on your work or school schedule, commuting time, and other factors, but quantifying the allocation of time with the most basic components of our lives gives a starting point for choosing the allocations that make sense for us. When we choose with purpose and commit to those activities, tasks, and efforts that support our values and goals, we live intentionally and become less susceptible to distractors that sabotage our intentions. Still, prioritizing among a set of choices is difficult but not impossible. Using our list as litmus test helps us evaluate what is most important in terms of our values and goals.

Large organizations have incorporated this concept into their company strategies by articulating the company vision, values, and mission, then crafting strategic and tactical plans to carry out those intentions. When I worked as a software developer, the company collected client enhancement requests as input into the next eighteen-month development cycle. Common requests rose to the top of the development priorities list, and unique items were often deferred until the next cycle. Some requests never made it into the development pipeline. Programming resources were dedicated only to the specific enhancements deemed critical to the product. Similarly, as the CEO of company YOU, deliberately choose and focus on your core values. Plan your efforts and divide your time in relative proportion to your personal mission. If your work values include, for example, customer service, new business, and staff development, their relative importance can be quantified as a guide for how best to allocate available time. Using this method, one account manager broke down her vision:

- Customer service: 50 percent

- New business development: 30 percent

- Staff development: 20 percent

Doing this established a basis of how to manage her time. When, after reviewing the past month work schedule, she noticed she spent many days wholly on customer service, she realized that carving out specific hours for staff development and new business within a day was unrealistic. Instead, she intentionally planned specific days for these activities to better enable her to dedicate days to customer service without undermining her efforts for supporting staff and new business.

Whether at work or at home, take these steps to optimize your schedule:

✓ Identify two to three goals.

✓ Identify three to four priorities for a given period

(adjust time as appropriate).

✓ Measure all tasks against priorities and goals.

✓ Arrange your schedule deliberately.

✓ Balance tough work with easier work for a mental break.

✓ Attend to priority tasks first.

✓ Fit lower priority tasks into any calendar gaps.

✓ Use blocks of time in minimum of forty-five-minute increments.

✓ Consider delegating tasks to others.

✓ Anticipate busy times and plan accordingly:

- Defer lower priority tasks until later.

- Plan breaks.

- Avoid scheduling discretionary activities during peak times.

Optimizing Your Workday

For office workers and professionals worldwide, the workday is driven by a calendar, whether an old-school day planner, a monthly chart posted on an office wall, an e-calendar such as Outlook, or a desk blotter inked with meetings and appointments. Once you have identified your core vision and relative importance (in percentages), the next step is to identify your work tasks. Consider all that you do within your job, listing out each as a line item. Common job items may include the following:

- checking email

- calls (with clients, vendors, etc.)

- staff meetings

- known deadlines (i.e., weekly reports)

- regular recurring meetings

- recurring deadlines (i.e., month-end reconciliation)

- recurring tasks

- training

For each of these in your list of work tasks, first estimate the percentage of how important each is, compared to other work tasks you typically do. Then evaluate the percentage relative to other tasks and adjust the breakdown for feasibility and reality. This is tricky because we poorly estimate how long tasks actually take to complete. Though we may want to spend more time on-site with our customers, the reality may be that we spend more time in the office. An objective reflection of desired versus actual time spent is necessary. Some people find it helpful to monitor the length of time for each task by tracking it manually for one or two typical work weeks; they are often surprised at how long they actually spend doing various things. It can be done rather easily by recording in a calendar app using a brief note every thirty minutes throughout the day. (See chapter 10 for an activity-tracking exercise.) Tracking tasks manually may be tedious, but the time and effort is worthwhile because it provides real numbers to work with, not just guesstimates. Those numbers then show the reality of task length. For example, if checking emails is a regular part of your day, you may estimate it takes up forty-five minutes of your morning. However, tracking manually over a two-week period may reveal some unexpected differences from your projections, for example, (1) you check email frequently throughout the day, not just every morning, and (2) cumulatively the time spent adds up to ninety minutes daily.

Had you tried to allocate your workday tasks based on the estimate of forty-five minutes checking email, your schedule will already be forty-five minutes behind each day. Once you have the tasks accurately measured for length of time spent, evaluate these in terms of your priorities. Every task or activity does not hold the same relative value. Pick three to four top priorities. Of those, your allocated time for these should be relatively greater than for the lower priority tasks.

Sheila is an attorney with a staff of eight junior partners, paralegals, and administrative professionals. Her main priorities at work are maximum billable hours, court time, and developing an effective team culture. She spends her weeks on tasks as follows:

- new client/case intake calls

- case work

- managing staff

- reviewing staff work

- staff meetings

- dictating letters

- in court

- partner meetings

- billable time entry

- professional society activity

- answering emails

- client/referral calls

Sheila created estimates for how much time she spends on each of these in a given week. Since her work week varies by whether she is in court, her schedule has considerable variation. She found it helpful to quantify all office activities and not the court time to discern where her office time was going. Tracking revealed considerably more time spent reviewing staff work and answering questions than she had estimated. With the new knowledge of how these management activities cut into her billable case hours, Sheila made decisions to create a new leadership role within her team to delegate some of the management work she was currently doing herself. This not only alleviated time pressures on Sheila, it provided a career development opportunity for a top performer on her team, created a backup resource for when Sheila was in court, and allowed timely response to questions and work to proceed without delays.

For those not in a management role, the tracking exercise is useful in demonstrating your current work balance. After you refine it and work out a plan to align with your priorities, it is a good idea to also review this plan with your boss. The boss may have other priorities in mind and can help you determine where to better exert your effort. The boss can also alleviate the burden of difficult choices when you are unsure which demand takes priority. Evaluating any possible tasks against your true values and goals, along with your boss's priorities, offers critical input for objectively defining where to allocate your time. It enables you to create order out of chaos. Knowing your regular activities and their priorities and urgency allows you to develop routine.

Stress often stems from uncertainty and a lack of control. When routine is introduced in a schedule, stress is reduced because you control when you do what. This feeling of being able to exert control and make decisions for yourself is considered one of the three basic psychological needs—autonomy. When routine is built into your day or week, some tasks become automatic. For example, I check email for forty-five minutes as soon as I arrive at work; I keep an open door for my team to ask questions or bring in work to review every day for the half hour before lunch. Regardless of the eccentricities of any schedule, there are always some opportunities to create regularity and routine. Though every day may be different, perhaps court days and office days each have a separate schedule template that can be applied. Mondays and Wednesdays may always be on a similar schedule, while Tuesday and Thursday vary, and Friday is a travel day. Tracking your activities over a period of a couple weeks allows you to discover patterns and opportunities to create regularity—making order out of chaos.

Optimizing Personal Time

As with a workday, your personal time can also be optimized, and routine can be created out of chaos. Routine is your best friend in time management. Having routine frees your brain to exert effort elsewhere—on more important things—and prevents getting bogged down with logistics. In your personal life, routine allows you to also establish a regular schedule for sleep, waking up, exercise, health, leisure, and social activities. We can borrow the same techniques used for maximizing a work week. Identify all the various activities you do in your personal time, such as the following:

- sleep

- meals

- family time

- exercise

- hobbies

- help with homework

- volunteering

- downtime

- personal appointments (medical, grooming, financial, etc.)

As an employee might optimize a workday, the same exercise of estimating the importance of each personal activity relative to the others and then recording how much time you currently spend on each can be applied. Tracking these over a two-week period provides actual numbers for task length. Review the actual length of time spent against your predetermined relative importance. Make adjustments so that your time allocation reflects your values. This practice often identifies surprising imbalances, providing insights you can apply to creating a better plan.

Other basic practices ensure you stay on top of your calendar:

✓ Set aside one day each week to review the upcoming week's demands and plan and adjust your calendar. Factor in any special happenings and adjust accordingly.

✓ Think of yourself as an athlete with a training schedule. Just as athletes have particular events they strive for—winning the big game, breaking a personal record—consider your calendar as your training schedule. If you have ever trained for a 5K run, you know there are training schedules templates available to follow so that in eight to ten weeks you can run three miles. Let your calendar be the recipe for successfully managing time and working toward your goals.

✓ Create regularity. In establishing patterns of time usage, we develop a cadence or rhythm to our days and weeks. This regularity becomes a calming force in an otherwise chaotic world. Try to avoid every day having a completely different schedule, even if that means there are only a few hours where there is continuity across days.

✓ Exercise discipline in following a schedule; practice making informed choices. Try out a schedule for a period of time before making changes. Your schedule can become a habit as well. It takes twenty-one consecutive days or more to develop (or break) a habit. The more habitual your schedule becomes, the more you free your mind up to focus on the important things, and the less you need to attend to the logistics of daily life. Stick to it!

✓ Pick a single method or technology and use it exclusively. Whether manual or virtual, your method should encompass all your time demands and be portable. It must be available to you at any point, anywhere, whether that means you carry it with you or it is accessible via the cloud. (Chapter 11 explores technology to support managing time and priorities.)

These techniques are recommendations and are not meant to be inflexible and rigid. It is crucial to remain flexible and periodically reevaluate to ensure you are not being driven by outdated goals and incorrect assumptions. By periodically reviewing and refining your schedule as necessary, it becomes a sustainable habit which supports you in creating the life you want.

Priorities Exercise

In this exercise, you will explore the current challenges you face in managing time and priorities and then create your personal values and goals list against which to measure current demands competing for your time and attention.

In setting your priorities, values, and goals, it is helpful to consider the big picture of your life, including home, work, and interests. Sometimes it is useful to start with a long-term vision of where you would like to be in a six-month, one-year, or three-year time frame (or shorter for students), then with that in mind you can focus on the immediate focus for the near term. In the chapter example, Mai was looking at a three- to six-month time frame of specific goals in the context of overall life values such as family time. In articulating your list, use positive, forward language and avoid statements that focus on what you don't want.

If your priorities and time management struggles are primarily work-related, for this exercise you can confine your list to work goals and activities. If work-life balance is your main concern, your list may include more values than goals.

1. *Values*—Think about what is truly important to you. Identify those values that will require some dedication of your time and energy. Consider the big picture—life values are more like a long-term investment. Some examples include reconnecting with extended family, contributing your talents to the community through meaningful volunteer work with a youth organization, or developing a career in financial technology. Be as specific as possible. Write down a few of these.

2. *Goals*—Think about what you want to accomplish over the next three to six months. (Time frame can be adjusted based on your situation. For example, students may shorten this in accordance with an academic term.) Articulate these goals in succinct, specific, actionable language. Some examples could include developing your thesis proposal, drafting a business plan, or joining a charitable organization. These should directly correspond to the values you noted above.

3. *Top priority*—Pick the three to five statements from your values and goals lists above that are most critical for this time period. Create your litmus test list against which you will evaluate demands for your time and energy. It is not necessary to tackle all goals at once, and those that do not make your final list now can be reserved for later. Giving ourselves a chance to build success with only one to two key goals initially builds our confidence in managing priorities while developing time management skills.

4. *Visualize*—Write your refined list out on notecards and post them prominently where you will see them regularly—on your bathroom mirror, keyboard tray, refrigerator, or car visor. Or post them electronically on your screensaver, phone background, or the app of your choice. The idea is to have the list readily available for you to check *before* saying yes to requests, adding another task, or booking another engagement.

Remember Mai's story and how she used her list to determine whether or not to take the cooking class with her friend. You, too, can use your list in the same way, as a means to evaluate the worthiness of a demand against your true values and the goals you set out to achieve.

CHAPTER 10
In a Time Warp: The Perception of Time

The study of perception in psychology in the past had been limited to sensory studies of hearing, vision, touch, taste, and smell. Sensory organs dedicated to receiving specific types of stimuli became relatively easy targets for lab work and medical science. Time, however, is not perceived by a single sensory organ but rather by a complex multifunctional organ, the brain. Multiple regions of the brain are involved in sensing time, including the cerebellum, hippocampus, basal ganglia, frontal cortex, and parietal cortex. The neural processes of time perception are also mediated by memory, attention, emotion, and even disease. While scientists have yet to agree on a model for time perception in the central nervous system, a few findings inform our current best practice for managing and using our time.

Studies involving decision-making and choice, multitasking, and attention indicate how we can make better use of our time and manage our thoughts about tasks, work, and focus. This chapter gives readers practical techniques for handling interruptions, transitioning between tasks, scheduling activity based on the body's circadian rhythms, and blocking time for focused attention. By developing better time habits, creating routine, and making use of the flow state of consciousness, we are better able to get what's important done. Since our memory, attention, and emotions are involved in perceiving time, it is important to consider how we *experience* rather than *spend* our time.

One of the biggest disruptions to our experience of time has to do with our body's circadian rhythms, the cyclic changes to the body, brain, and behavior in response to light and darkness in the environment. Many body functions are driven by our circadian rhythms, including wake and sleep patterns, release of hormones, body temperature, and digestion. Interference with our natural circadian rhythms can result in various health conditions or disease states. Our sleep cycle is one of the most visible manifestations of our circadian rhythm, or internal clock.

Yet, sleep deprivation and irregular hours of wakefulness are all too common among busy working adults. Some people tout their minimal hours of sleep as if it were a badge of honor, though it is known that lack of sleep contributes to high blood pressure, cardiovascular disease, obesity, and depression. We know that quality sleep is critical to the formation of new memories, learning, concentration, and response time. Sleep deprivation can also lead to symptoms of ADD and ADHD in those without the condition. So if becoming too busy and poorly managing all the demands on our time means something's got to give, that sacrificial lamb should be something other than our precious sleep. Sleep is one area of our life we can control; it is a necessary and important behavior that should not be relegated to whatever time is left over in our day. A simple yet underutilized practice is to plan your sleep schedule just as you would your work tasks and other commitments. Poor concentration, inability to focus, drowsiness, and indecisiveness resulting from lack of sleep will impact any important tasks you had on the calendar, likely costing you precious hours correcting careless mistakes. We can avoid this pitfall by making quality sleep a priority every night.

Another key factor in managing time is to identify how and when we are at our best, considering our own internal clock and body rhythms. There is really an art to designing one's own best schedule. Only you know what your peak times of day are, that is, when you work best and are most mentally sharp. Use this awareness to leverage your best performance when it counts. Ideally, aim to create a schedule that maximizes your attention and strengths.

Engage in some reflection about the demands on your time and your internal rhythms:

- When is your best time of day to learn, work, and study?

- When do you have the most trouble attending or focusing?

- What are your interactive activities (such as work presentations or spoken language classes)?

- What are your passive activities (such as work meetings or lecture classes)?

- Do night activities or classes make sense for you in terms of your physical alertness?

- What similar daily tasks and activities do you have that can be stacked together?

- If you take medications, how do the meds affect you throughout the day?

Knowing the answers to these questions helps us craft a schedule that works best for our needs and positions us to create that regularity and routine. If you work best early in the morning, late afternoon, or just before lunch, take advantage of this by scheduling your most critical or mentally demanding work at those times. Choices exist for when we should do what needs to be done and how to allocate time during our workday or in our school schedule.

For students, that may mean spreading classes over five days rather than a heavy class load on some days and no classes on others, foregoing night classes due to late-day fatigue. For an executive, it may mean using mornings, when she is most mentally sharp, for creative and detail work, with meetings stacked throughout the afternoon. If you tend to be a bit foggy after lunch, this could be a time for easier tasks like paperwork, time tracking, billing, or the pass-fail class in a college schedule. After lunch could become the designated workout period, eliminating mental demands and restoring physical energy through exercise. Interactive activities that require engagement are best scheduled when we are sharp and able to be fully present, not when we are drained or preoccupied. For a working parent, that may mean helping your kids with homework after dinner instead of upon arriving home from work. If your energy wanes in the evening, that may not be the best time for your online class or for putting in extra hours to catch up on work. Instead, consider an earlier start to your day or using weekend mornings to optimize your focus.

Stacking similar activities allows us to get in a certain mindset and minimize lost time in transition. For example, if you have regular health appointments each month, it is less disruptive to take a few hours off one afternoon and get them all in than to dart out for appointments multiple times. (More about transitions later.) If your work schedule requires meetings with individual staff members to assess work progress, stacking these successively over a period of time economizes your schedule and also creates a routine your staff observes as well. And lastly, your physical attention and energy may vary throughout the day as a result of medications you may take, and accounting for the impact on your focus can help you utilize your attention more effectively.

Multitasking and Interruptions

Do you sometimes feel like the subject in a cubist Picasso painting, fragmented, displaced, and pulled apart in many directions? When demands are numerous, we tend to resort to multitasking as a solution. While we think of multitasking as a way to get many things done at once, in reality the human brain cannot multitask when managing thoughts. The brain cannot hold two simultaneous thoughts, and what we think of as multitasking is really an illusion; our brain quickly shifts attention back and forth between two targets. I remind my clients that multitasking is way overrated. It is a delusion that robs us of efficacy and prohibits being fully present. The brain, in switching back and forth between thoughts, expends energy in recalling and processing each thought every time the switch occurs. Doing several things at once robs each task of your full attention! Even simpler multitasking, such as speaking on the phone while reviewing a report on your desk, exhausts the brain prematurely. If you are already having attention challenges due to end-of-the-day fatigue, disinterest, hunger, or poor sleep the night before, multitasking can put you over the edge. The hard truth is that undivided attention for less time is more effective than multitasking to accomplish many tasks at once.

Transitions

Attention is controlled within the brain by a complex interaction of neural networks involving neurotransmitters for alerting (norepinephrine) and orienting (acetylcholine), genetics, and environmental factors. Attentional behavior is present in infants, yet changes occur through maturation into adulthood. The brain must regulate conflicting cognitive tasks, modulate switching between tasks, inhibit distractors, exercise decision-making, and control emotion when attending.[19] Recent research emphasizes the importance of the ability to filter out superfluous stimuli, in addition to traditional views of attention regulation regarding the brain's ability to focus. MRI studies in which areas of the brain are measured show that interventions and learning can influence brain changes as attentional behaviors are learned. While neuroscientists are just beginning to understand the intricate regulators of attention, it is clear that it involves brain development throughout childhood into adulthood and relies on learned behaviors.

A common challenge in managing time and priorities is the ability to switch between cognitive tasks. When we go from reading a scientific paper, for example, to performing a statistical analysis, different cognitive skills are called up and suppressed within the brain. When we change from one work task to another, our brain must relinquish attention from the first one and prepare for the next.

We must ramp up for the upcoming work and diminish attention on the outgoing task. These transitions cost mental effort and require expenditure of energy for regulation of our attention. To the extent that we can minimize and eliminate unnecessary transitions, we conserve precious brain power and reap the benefit of sustained attention. Interruptions can be considered unnecessary transitions. They require us to relinquish attention on one cognitive task and divert it to another. As with transitions between differing cognitive tasks, interruptions cost time and brain power. They require the momentary reorientation to the interruption source and after the interruption, require a ramping up to the previous cognitive task. Think of how often we utter "Now where was I?" when resuming work after an interruption. "Where was I?" is a manifestation of the brain ramping up to cognitively resume the task at hand. These instances involve some backtracking, as the most recent thoughts immediately preceding the distraction may not have had sufficient processing to commit to memory. Clearly the inefficiencies of interruptions are readily observed.

Consider the following: Mario, a software engineer, set aside three hours on Monday afternoon to work through a system error his users were getting at a particular point in the inventory system. In testing for the error, he tried multiple navigation paths and system functions to emulate the user's actions but was having difficulty recreating the error himself. He determined that a specific combination of system events must lead to this error and set out to test multiple iterations of path combinations to isolate the occurrence. This effort required painstaking, deliberate exercise of variants and considerable concentration to effectively rule out scenarios in which the error did not occur. Seventy minutes into this, a team member entered his office with a pressing issue that needed Mario's direction. They discussed the issue and options and concluded with a path forward for the team member to resolve it. During the twenty minutes of the impromptu meeting, Mario abruptly switched gears from iterative testing scenarios to the immediate problem presented by his team member. Now, resuming his testing, Mario had to reestablish just where he had stopped, get back into the problem-solving and testing mode, and review his notes to ascertain which test scenario he had last run. The interruption cost not just twenty minutes but also the cognitive load of ramping back up to resume. Having tested for seventy minutes before the intrusion, Mario had been "in the zone" working effectively at peak performance. It would take some time to get back in that high performance mode upon resuming the original task. The three hours allotted for testing was reduced to less than two and a half hours given the unplanned interruption and transition. Several interruptions over a day result in a significant cumulative loss of productive time.

Mario's testing example illustrates the impact of minimizing transitions and interruptions within our schedules. Though we may have the best intentions on how to manage our time, our actions are not always consistent with those intentions. Mario had intended to dedicate three hours to the error testing. He blocked out time to do so but failed to take steps to ensure this time was preserved. What could have been done to preserve the allotted period?

For any adult worker or student, there are several ways interruptions can be minimized:

✓ *Physically* distance yourself.

✓ Determine how, when, and where you work best.

✓ Establish an organized workspace.

✓ Identify and utilize alternative work locations.

✓ Hold all calls, and silence your phone.

✓ *Virtually* distance yourself.

Physical distance from coworkers is easy if you have your own office. Simply close the door. Some people are less likely to knock on a closed door than if the door is wide open. A closed door indicates a need for privacy or uninterrupted work. Without having your own office, however, you can give yourself distance by scheduling time to work in a conference room on your floor with the door closed, finding a quiet spot in an open-concept office away from group work areas, or scheduling a work-from-home day if your company allows. Ask your supervisor for suggested locations to work quietly. Students can use a study carrel or find the quietest sublevel stacks in the library to physically isolate themselves for study. Headphones are helpful to virtually distance us and dampen audio distractions from nearby office chatter. Nearby coffee shops or the company cafeteria can offer a quiet work alternative location at off-peak times. Perhaps you regularly go to the office library whenever you have detailed reports to review. Alternative locations can provide not only a change of pace but a mental cue for productivity when used regularly for the same kind of tasks. Sometimes it helps to dedicate a specific space for a specific type of activity. The brain learns to associate that particular space with a specific task, acclimating to a location-task mindset to more readily focus on the task at hand. Only you know how, when, and where you work best.

Your own desk can be fraught with distractions that interrupt your thinking and detract from concentrated work time. Take time to declutter your desk and plan a time to do so weekly so you are not tempted by the mounting piles of paperwork, mail, or that office plant that needs pruning.

Virtual distancing can also reduce the impact of ever-present chatter from our online world. The ubiquity of Wi-Fi and portability of the very technology that keeps us connected also sometimes works against a single focus, instead enticing us toward multitasking. We must be mindful of when it is appropriate and makes sense to use these tools despite their high accessibility and always-on availability. The onus falls on us as users of technology to rein in the viselike grip it holds on us. Turn off phone notifications, such as news, sports, and stock market alerts, which momentarily steal your attention as the alert appears. You can decide when to check these and even plan a set time of day to get the latest, without allowing these notices to interrupt you real-time as events unfold. Applications like LinkedIn, Twitter, and even email can be configured to turn off notifications and give you a vibration-free block of time. You decide when to check these, how often to check, or whether to check them at all. Apps like Facebook, Twitter, Pinterest, LinkedIn, Instagram, TikTok, or email can be all-consuming. A more effective way to manage these is to limit their use to a set period per day with few exceptions. This goes back to the idea of *you* determining what is important to you and actively controlling your attention and priorities. Though I keep current with industry news and research publications through online platforms, I found it was not necessary to be notified every time one of my peers published an article, commented on a post, or was celebrating a work anniversary. By setting aside a set time in my weekly calendar to check on the latest from my online communities (and configuring apps to turn off certain notifications altogether), I didn't miss out on important happenings and spared myself countless interruptions day and night.

Block Party

Successful people, whether at work or school, block out regular productive periods in their busy schedules for high priority work. Psychologists recommend taking short mental and physical breaks after fifty minutes of concentrated effort. A healthy application of these two principles involves setting aside two-hour increments of time to devote to a particular task, taking a short break midway into it, which could be used to stand up and stretch, get coffee, move around, or simply step outside. This habit leads to great productivity while optimizing both physical and mental well-being, leading to a sustainable practice that can be made part of any ongoing schedule. Blocking time into two-hour increments allows significant progress to occur on a given task and is a feasible practice for chunking a schedule into reasonable units. Blocking out time supports getting many things done. During the two-hour blocks, it is important to minimize interruptions. Defer anything unrelated to the blocked task until after the entire block has passed. In designing a schedule with blocks, we can fill in the gaps with smaller, less intense activities such as returning calls, running occasional errands, or tackling those pesky tasks that arise unexpectedly.

Do not check messages, take calls, or allow notifications or interruptions during dedicated block time. Blocks should also coincide with your peak times of day, based on your biorhythms. Once again, the basic premise is to *choose* and *plan* time for the important things. Block out generous two-hour chunks of time for similar tasks, even though they may be comprised of several discrete tasks with a five- or ten-minute break in between.

For example, copy editor Kris uses a two-hour block to review several articles for the upcoming week's publication. Though each article may only require a half hour to edit, the two-hour block allows Kris the ability to dedicate brain power for those tasks requiring similar mental effort, minimizing any ramping up.

Use consecutive blocks for lengthy units of work. In planning a schedule with two-hour increments, we become proactive. If it turns out that you don't need the full two hours for a block, it can be used to do something else, take an impromptu break, or complete the so-called gap-filler tasks that require only minimal focus and little time. By blocking time into two-hour increments whenever possible, we minimize the mental energy and stress associated with transitioning our focus from one activity to another.

Being self-employed, I plan my own schedule. I conduct individual coaching sessions and workshops, work days on-site for corporate clients, research and review studies, and write for blogs and publications. I have a variety of activities to manage within my work week. Whenever possible, I block out two-hour increments to allow my brain to get into writing mode, research mode, client mode, presentation mode, and so on.

It boils down to *intentionally choosing* how we experience time. Once I get into my writing mode, I have saved the extraneous mental effort and energy I might have spent getting settled in and getting my materials ready; I am set for a period of time. It's like learning to drive a car with manual transmission. Switching gears takes a bit of effort, but once the car is in fourth gear it can cruise smoothly for a while. Similarly, once you get into gear with your various work modes, you can focus better, maintain a cognitive continuity, cruise along, and not experience the hassles of transition.

Blocking time is a way to increase the opportunity to establish a flow state, a highly focused state of consciousness known for productivity, described by psychologist Mihaly Csikszentmihalyi. A flow state is conducive to working at our optimal performance, being "in the zone" (see chapter 13). When we block out time, we begin to create a sustainable strategy for managing our priorities and controlling our focus.

Working in healthcare for many years and developing hospital scheduling software, I have seen first-hand many complex schedules, such as those for the allocation of operating rooms for scheduled and emergency cases, outpatient care, and imaging diagnostic services. Often the most challenging part of implementing a computerized scheduling system is for its users to establish their scheduling priorities and create rules to govern their time. Physicians often split time between surgical cases, office visits, rounds, and follow-up. Surgeons have long employed the practice of blocked time for surgery (and blocked time for golf). A surgeon's schedule may reveal that every Tuesday 6 a.m. to 2 p.m. is reserved for surgery. Because of her contractual arrangement with the hospital and its operating room availability, she cannot do patient appointments at that time, cannot be interrupted, and will not be returning calls during that period because she is physically in the operation room. A rule is set that cannot be broken. Mondays, Wednesdays, and Fridays are allocated for patient visits, with further refinement for new patient consultations and follow-up visits. Afternoon hours are dedicated for consults with other physicians. Medical professionals often rely on others to book their schedule and, as a result, have had to set rules for how their time will be allocated since others are managing their calendar. The discipline in defining block periods allows medical professionals to accomplish a great deal in a limited amount of time. We can all learn from their practices. To establish "block parties," follow these basic rules:

- ✓ Define two-hour increments with a ten-minute break midway.
- ✓ Minimize transitions—allow time to get in the zone.
  - Transitions cost time and are inefficient.
  - Build fewer transitions into your schedule.
- ✓ Aim for a flow state for peak performance.
- ✓ Fill in gaps with lower priority items.

Creating a Schedule

Creating your own unique schedule involves some basic building blocks, regardless of what tool you use to keep a schedule. Whether electronic or on paper, any schedule begins with an open slate and can be developed using this five-step approach:

1. Start with the knowns. As in solving an algebraic problem, first identify all the "knowns" in your day. Start at a high level with broad strokes and create shape within the days, with periods dedicated to given priorities that cannot be eliminated. We all must sleep and eat. Consider your normal sleep requirements, for example, eight hours, and the remaining time is schedulable time. While some may forego three meals a day, generally it is good to allot time for meals, even if only twenty minutes for breakfast and lunch and slightly longer for dinner. If sleep and mealtimes are not baked in, your calendar will start off behind.

   If you are working, identify your work hours, whether it is a forty-hour work week over five days, three twelve-hour shifts every seven days, or another set schedule. For students, a school schedule becomes the work week. Identify class and study schedules for each day of the week. The work week creates regular (long) blocks within a schedule. Around these broad ranges, we build in our other knowns, such as our commuting time, regular medical appointments, daycare drop-off and pickup times. Build in times for family commitments, which may fall outside of the work/school hours.

2. Refer back to your values and goals list (from chapter 9) and record periods dedicated to each of these. The values list

becomes a source for overall goals that may translate into specific must-do tasks.

3. Designate time for more specific activities within the broad range of work/school hours. Note any deadlines, regular meetings, project milestones, exam dates—any committed specific dates. Break out specific time blocks to address these items. Fill in blocks for all the work/school tasks you must do. Ask yourself, "Is this a must or a want?" Schedule time for all the musts. (We will come back to the wants later.) Schedule specific times for checking email, returning calls, social media, and other regular activities that may not have a clearly defined endpoint but require your attention. Choose specific amounts of time to allocate for these. Recalling the blocking principle, try to minimize transitions by allocating blocks of time in two-hour increments.

4. Create time for scheduled breaks. Build in time for renewal and downtime with nothing specific planned. While this seems counterintuitive to managing time, downtime allows us to restore our reserves and resume concentrated effort with a refreshed and energized state of mind. Breaks prime the pump for more productive work time.

5. Add in time for the "extras." Time for exercise, health, social life, and leisure activities is not really expendable and should not be regarded as extra. These behaviors are vital to our well-being. Recalling how powerfully language influences our thoughts, we must stop referring to these important well-being necessities as extra. Without making time for

these, our productivity is diminished, we cannot work at optimal levels, and our well-being suffers. Allow some time for some of these activities every day. Family time, exercise, social engagements, hobbies, and scheduled appointments can all fall into this category. While it is important to schedule time for these activities, there is frequently an opportunity to be more flexible with these. For example, you can designate a hair appointment as tentative and reschedule it if you decide to work late that evening. There will always be time commitments you can defer, forego, or override as necessary.

6. Allow for the unplanned. By allowing time for the unplanned—that empty space in our schedule—we avoid leaving ourselves so booked that spontaneity or flexibility is lost. By simply keeping those unplanned items to a limited time, we can get back to our plan with little repercussion.

Creating a schedule is often a work in progress. When you take the first step and start crafting a schedule, you will surely find that some refinements are necessary. We inherently underestimate how long things actually take, and after trying a schedule for a bit we discover those realities and must readjust. That's okay! To be useful, the schedule must be realistic and sustainable, and by tweaking it with learned observations, your schedule starts working for you and not against you. We can refine actual lengths of time by recording a note in the calendar next to the scheduled item, indicating the true amount of time. By reviewing these notes weekly, we can compare actual to planned amount of time, and this informal quantitative exercise reveals meaningful insights that guide our future planning.

Often transit time is overlooked and we fail to account for any prep time needed between activities. It is helpful to actually record these separate from the task itself. In coaching clients to better manage their time and priorities, I recommend they do activity tracking for a period of at least two weeks using the activity log below.

Setbacks

Everyone experiences setbacks from time to time. These are great opportunities to learn from our mistakes in planning and identify points from which to pivot to a new approach or better plan. Too often, we let setbacks derail us entirely, and we fail to salvage anything useful from our original intentions. Look closely at what is and isn't working, make changes as needed, and get right back into using a better schedule.

There are also the inevitable interruptions that can thwart the best intentions. For an unexpected call that gets through or from someone you designated as a priority contact, if the issue is not urgent, arrange a time to call them back when you are free and able to devote your attention. There will be times in your schedule that you have designated as downtime and small gaps between tasks. Those gaps are then available to be used to address the unexpected.

Managing our priorities is a learned skill. Practicing some of the techniques to better choose how we spend our time produces better results. Use setbacks as learning opportunities and thereby continuously improve your planning abilities. We learn to work smarter, not harder.

Managing Expectations

Our success in managing our priorities and schedule can benefit from enlisting the help of others. Make your availability known to your coworkers, significant others, or children, sharing calendars or communicating important schedule items. This helps others know the best times to reach you and when you are unavailable, and they can plan accordingly. Share your schedule on a need-to-know basis. It is important to manage your own expectations and that of others around you. We cannot do it all and be well. Other people cannot know our priorities unless we share it with them. By sharing with those important to us, we empower ourselves to make good choices without misrepresenting our intentions. Informing others of scheduling challenges or conflicts creates the opportunity to engage them in finding a solution. Sharing our priorities and interests with others provides insight into our scheduling choices. While they may disagree with our priorities, it becomes clear why there is little room in the schedule or why a request must be delayed. It may be necessary to advocate for yourself, with your boss, your partner, or others if conflicts arise. We must become our own self-advocate. We are empowered when we give ourselves the gift of time and focus.

Activity Log Time Management Exercise

The Activity Log will enable you to see how you actually spend time over a given two-week period. Through awareness of how you currently spend your time, you can begin to identify patterns that may or may not be supporting your goals. For example, you may find, after reviewing your two-week log, that you are actually spending twelve hours a week in administrative meetings or on prospect calls when you had originally estimated and planned to dedicate only six hours per week to this activity. Or you may see that you spend only six and a quarter hours per day with clients instead of your planned eight hours due to interruptions from phone calls and unplanned activities.

After two weeks of tracking the activity log, you will discover some practices that you may decide to change *and* for which you have the ability to change. To live the intentional living model, we start with discovery. We find our intentions often do not match reality, putting us further behind and diverting our attention and energies toward less important tasks. Once you see just how different what *you intend* to do is from what you *actually* do, you can apply the model. When we identify how long units of work actually take based on the quantitative data we collect, we can then take informed action. We can better support our goals through deliberate choice and strategies. By documenting sources of distractions and what actually occurs during a given period, we can discern novel ways to mitigate diversions and readjust our schedule with realistic insights. Awareness is the first step toward behavior change.

Follow these instructions to track your activities in preparation for creating a schedule:

1. Record all your activities for a two-week period using the spreadsheet (printed or online; see figure 10.1 for an example of a spreadsheet). Be honest!

2. It is best to keep the log with you or on your computer or smartphone and make a note at least every hour, preferably in thirty-minute increments, as to how you spent that time.

3. Use no less than fifteen-minute time intervals. (Break times may be an exception.)

4. Track from when you begin your workday to when you end your workday (including your commute times) for weekdays; record weekend days only if you work. (The log can be modified to accommodate other hours or days for your personal schedule if that is an area you wish to improve.)

5. Be detailed enough to identify specific tasks at the unit level if possible; phrases or categories of work are okay to use, but also specify any details (i.e., meeting—staff, meeting—executive, meeting—offsite, meeting—J. Smalls).

6. Shorthand or quick notes are fine as long as you can discern the meaning. Be honest!

7. You can adjust the time intervals on the spreadsheet to fit your workday and increments that best fit your schedule. Or if you have a time-keeping system in place, you can use that as a record provided it has sufficient detail. However, do not just copy your iCalendar or Outlook calendar. Our purpose is to look at actual time not planned time.

8. After your two weeks of recording workday activities, review this to discover patterns and surprises. Circle any discrepancies between time planned and actual time spent for any task. Circle any unplanned tasks that were added into your day. Add up time spent for the same activity over a period of one week. Compare this total to your planned time for this activity. Note any unplanned activities and calculate a total for those.

For example, Hope had allowed a half hour daily upon arriving at work for checking email. In reviewing her activity log, she found that on most days she actually spent fifty to sixty-five minutes checking email. In a one-week period, instead of her planned two and a half hours on email, she spent nearly six hours on email.

9. From your own log, you will discover insights and identify opportunities for improving your schedule and better prioritizing your efforts to support your intentions. Add time for those activities that consistently took longer than anticipated. Block out time for unplanned activities, or allow enough room for unexpected tasks to be factored in. The insights gained in this exercise allow you to better plan your future schedule using quantitative data rather than your gut feeling or hunch. The activity log exercise can be used anytime you feel your schedule is getting out of control to refine and adjust your plans. In Hope's case, the insight from her activity tracking showed her that she must allocate more time for email on a regular basis. She modified her schedule to allow for checking email one hour daily, cutting back in areas where she had overestimated the time required.

Figure 10.1: Activity log spreadsheet

WORK ACTIVITY LOG   Week of: _____

Time	SAMPLE -	MONDAY	TUESDAY	WEDNESDAY	THURSDAY	FRIDAY	Saturday	Sunday
7:00								
7:30	Check email							
8:00	Partner Meeting							
8:30	Partner Meeting							
9:00	Partner Meeting							
9:30	Return Phone Call							
10:00	Consult -J. Slaughter							
10:30	Webex: NYO							
11:00	Staff 1x1- Meg							
11:30	Staff 1x1- John							
12:00	Working Lunch - Case							
12:30	Working Lunch - Case							
1:00	Prep Brief: Smith							
1:30	Prep Brief: Smith							
2:00	Urgent call - Logicale acquisition							
2:30	Prep Brief: Smith							
3:00	Check Emails; Resp Deposition Date							
3:30	Travel							
4:00	Arbitration - Infonomics							
4:30	Arbitration - Infonomics							
4:45	Review: HYL Hearing							
5:30	Conference Call - County							
5:40	Check Emails							
6:00	Travel							
7:00	District Dinner Mtg							
7:30	District Dinner Mtg							
8:00								

CHAPTER 11
Cellphone, Smartwatch, Alexa:
There's an App for That!

Up until this point, we have explored how best to experience time and ways to ensure our priorities get the attention they deserve. Much of this involves choices to be made that are consistent with our intentions, values, goals, and desired lifestyle. Humans have been faced with the challenges of managing priorities and making deliberate choices for as long as they have roamed the earth. And, as we learned, the brain is not born with innate behaviors that optimize our experience of managing time. Learned behaviors improve our success in focusing on what is important.

Having the foundations for better time management and an understanding of how our brain influences our use of time, we can then employ technology to assist us with time and priorities. Electronic calendar best practices, cellphone features, and computer apps are best used when the fundamental time management principles are understood and applied. Several technology tools available today can enhance our ability to choose how time is spent, optimize our schedules, reduce and eliminate distractions, and free up more time for desired activities. With the associated discipline to apply best practice techniques and make deliberate choices, technology can be our friend. Without a commitment to established priorities, however, technology can easily become our downfall and worst enemy as an ever-present source of distractions and interruptions that drive us off course.

Technology must be viewed as a means to an end and a set of tools that enable us to produce a desired outcome. Today, technology has blurred the lines between many devices—cellphones, television, and computers—with increasingly device-independent apps made portable through the cloud. Many features can facilitate our navigation through life and work, while blurring the lines between workday and personal time. While clever apps can be enormously helpful, even indispensable to some, it is so important to choose the right ones and use them effectively. Regardless of which tool you use, get training on how best to use it.

Online tutorials are readily available for the do-it-yourself learner, while genius staff at the big box stores and mobile phone suppliers are there to help you in person. Many of these electronics gurus offer appointment scheduling for one-on-one help with your device. Basic and advanced features can be learned by watching how-to videos from the comfort of your living room. And there is always that reliable techie relative who can often clear up any confusion with a quick demonstration and personal instruction.

As a software developer early in my career and early adopter of mobile technology, I dreamed of the days when I would no longer have to cart around a phone, laptop, music player (CD or tape player), digital camera, personal digital assistant (PDA device, i.e., PalmPilot), and spiral notebook while traveling between client sites and my office. It was a giant step forward when the internet was accessible first to PDAs, and then smartphones with integrated cameras came into existence, thereby replacing multiple devices in the briefcase. Since the early 2000s, proliferation of countless applications to simplify our lives has, to some degree, confounded our ability to better manage life by introducing a magnitude of choice no one ever anticipated. Yet there are a few indispensable technologies that simplify our complicated lives.

Mobile Calendar

A mobile online calendar, such as Outlook, has become so indispensable to many of us, it is hard to imagine how we ever managed to get through a day before they came into being. By mobile calendar, I mean a calendar app that is cloud-based and therefore portable and accessible to you anywhere you go from any device. Not only offering a means of tracking appointments, today's mobile calendars allow you to do the following:

- ✓ record and update events and commitments all in one place

- ✓ schedule meetings and invite participants

- ✓ establish a virtual teleconference or conference call

- ✓ manage a to-do list

- ✓ maintain a list of contacts

- ✓ classify activities through color

- ✓ set up reminders

✓ designate activities as "private"

✓ switch between time zones

✓ reference or include email and associated documents

✓ maintain multiple calendars for various purposes

✓ share your calendar with colleagues and family

A great deal of information can and should be maintained in this one place—your online calendar. It is possible to keep one calendar for both work *and* home, for example. The mobile calendar allows for integration of each, and some people find the idea of everything for home and work in one place to be especially useful. A family calendar can be shared among Mom, Dad, and the kids, and even shared with Grandma, who transports children to and from activities. A work team can share calendars to ensure continuity of coverage or facilitate meeting scheduling.

Accessibility is what is perhaps the most impactful feature of a cloud-based calendar. If your boss wants to schedule an important dinner meeting with clients in June and your oldest child is graduating, you can easily double-check the graduation date to avoid a conflict by consulting the calendar on your phone, which your spouse thoughtfully loaded with important family dates shared from his calendar.

As a loyal cardholder of an American Express card since my college graduation, the company annually sent out high-quality leather planners, embossed with the cardholder's name and business, as a token of appreciation to its customers. These pocket-sized planners included not only calendar pages but world maps, time zones, units of measure tables, notes pages, and handy reference charts a businessperson might need. I looked forward to receiving one every year until about 2010, when I made a complete switch to a single electronic calendar. The portability of a system-based calendar (cloud technology was not yet available) proved invaluable and irreplaceable. There was no longer the worry of forgetting my book and even less need for a scheduling assistant in my office.

With a cloud-based calendar, portability and accessibility relies on internet access or mobile signal, which have become increasingly reliable worldwide. We can note all events, appointments, reminders, and notes, and pull them up anytime. We can add in time for work, fun, and the mundane. We can schedule using increments of our choosing. We can (and should) schedule in downtime, or free time. Applying our best practices of purposeful, intentional living, we choose how to spend our time, log it into the calendar, and *commit*.

Take Your Pick

Surprisingly, even the most successful leaders I work with often cite organizational skills as trouble areas that prevent them from achieving the goals they had set for themselves and their company. They lament a scarcity of time and resources. I remind them that time management is a learned skill, and most people do not consider improving their time management skills until they face problems resulting from poor time management. We typically explore the technology they are currently using and what does and doesn't work well for them. Occasionally, I find a leader who insists on relying on their own memory and who has chosen to forego use of a scheduling tool. Relying on our memory has inherent challenges and is not the best way to manage time.

Our brain makes mistakes. We have biases that influence what is remembered and how it may be remembered. There are errors of omission, duration, and perspective. It takes energy to remember— energy that could be put to better use elsewhere, especially when there are tools to do the remembering for us. A good leader can be a *better* leader with a good scheduling tool. Pick one from the many options out there, and use it exclusively. Learn how to use not only the basic features but also the more esoteric features, which may astound you with shortcuts and time savings you hadn't realized you need. Use the one tool for everything. Keep it current. Cloud technology, fortunately, has removed the need to sync calendars, as in prior app versions. Now once an item is entered, it is stored without further action. Use your scheduling tool to build your days and weeks with action that reinforces those values and goals salient to you. Schedule some downtime on a regular basis, if not daily. Share it with your important people. Do not rely on your memory. Free your memory for the important things.

Scheduling Tool Tips

For most people, it makes sense to use whatever scheduling app their workplace or school uses because it is usually integrated with email, document management, and other shared enterprise applications. You can then integrate this with your personal schedule by loading those activities into the calendar. Some apps allow you to designate personal appointments and suppress their display to anyone who may have access to your calendar at work. This keeps your personal and work activity separate and private if necessary.

If your workplace does not have a designated scheduling tool, ask your friends and other people what apps they use. You can also search online and explore various capabilities there. Once you have made a choice of app, start using it exclusively.

Let's look at a sample calendar for James, an attorney who uses Microsoft Outlook, shown in figure 11.1.

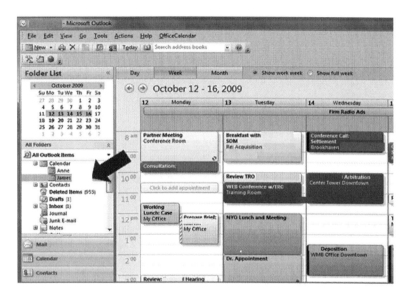

Figure 11.1: Sample Outlook calendar

Notice how James uses a lot of color coding so similar items can be viewed at a glance (i.e., in this image, light gray denotes staff meeting time, medium gray denotes project time, dark gray denotes external meetings, etc.). When making a calendar entry, the color can be set with your preferences to help you easily identify various types of activities at a glance.

Notice that on Monday, he is double-booked at noon, as shown by the overlapping appointments. The event *Prepare Brief* shows a striped left margin, indicating it is a tentative event. Marking items as *tentative* allows the event to be noted while alerting us that it may not occur and visually reminds us that something else could possibly be scheduled at the same time if necessary. Note also how much white space there is on this calendar. Not every time slot is filled. Open slots are planned. Empty space is actually good. It allows time for the unexpected or sudden demands that crop up and provides room if items run overtime. Empty space can be filled partially with the 'as time permits' tasks we want to do if possible. It also allows for downtime, which is important for restorative value.

On the left side of the screen, the other integrated features of Outlook are displayed. Note that other calendars can be selected (such as Anne's), and other folders, contacts, and emails can be accessed, becoming a virtual desktop exhibiting all facets related to the calendar. Many workers leave their calendar up all day long and just minimize it or layer it behind other work applications to keep it readily at hand to be called up as needed.

If you are new to the scheduling tool, this might look a bit overwhelming, but think of it as a recipe for your work week. With practice, commitment, and intentional decision-making, you will develop great time management skills that are enhanced by using technology.

Bells and Whistles

Once you become proficient at using a scheduling tool, there are additional ways to optimize your work schedule. I believe everyone needs a backup—someone to take over when they are out unexpectedly, become suddenly ill, or when the workload is greater than expected. We often underutilize the other people around us, forgetting about the intern who wants to learn, the quiet coworker who can lend a hand, or a more junior person who might shine given an opportunity. Leveraging the talent around us or delegating to others on our team are easy ways to build more time into our day. More time can also be found when we consider how well a job must be done. Some tasks, of course, must be exercised with perfection, though others could perhaps be approached with a sufficient mindset. It is important to recognize when perfection versus sufficient is necessary. The proposal for an expansive project with a new client warrants extra hours to completely convey your company's capabilities, whereas the email to your peers about an upcoming office move could be quickly crafted with sufficient detail without spending extra time on unnecessary fluff. This choice between *adequate* and *perfect* is often a source of surprise among leaders but surely makes an impact on their time commitments. Realizing which tasks can be completed with sufficient quality and which require perfection can be a breakthrough for busy people. It may also mean the difference between stress or burnout and peak performance.

A corollary to the sufficient versus perfect theorem is the practice of allocating tasks based on time available. If you truly have only one day to prepare the report, you must scale the work to fit the time constraints. Perhaps the report could be written better, made longer, or include additional material if there were two days to write it, yet sufficient quality must do if you have only one day to do it.

Choosing how to scale the work to fit the time is an art that can alleviate undue stress. When we recognize our limits, the constraints imposed, and the reality of a situation, it allows us to work within those confines with reduced stress.

Think of a couple who sets out to have a house built. They embark on a design, working with an architect and builder, holding grandiose ideals of a forever home that meets their current and future needs. Their desire to install exotic wood decking is thwarted by a three-month shipping delay from the supplier. Expedited shipping would cost an additional $3,500. When their budget, construction time frame, and materials lead time were factored in, they scaled back their design to one that is more feasible and realistic, using local materials. For work projects, too, realistically assessing work, time, and priorities facilitates proportionate allocation of work efforts to fit the time available. Doing so enables a sustainable, less stressful solution.

Avoid Reinventing the Wheel

Economy of scale is a useful concept in managing repetitive work or processes that are used again and again. For many occupations, projects comprise much of the work. Large projects, such as opening a new location in a retail chain, building a shopping center, or creating a new website, often involve a sequence of events and milestones that punctuate any similar project. There are specific courses and certifications for project management, and I will not attempt to condense that content here. However, several basic concepts of project management can be applied in our quest to better manage the workload of repetitive processes in our work.

Plan Ahead

Borrowing from your knowledge and experience with past projects, take time to identify the steps and sequence of the project through completion. Divide large bodies of work into smaller tasks or units of work. Schedule out milestones and checkpoints for various phases. Tentatively estimate resources (e.g., effort, equipment, tools) required for each unit and cumulative tasks within each phase. Identify contingencies that create dependency on completion of earlier units. Spread the work over the allotted time frame.

From critical path methods to Microsoft Project to Lean Six Sigma, many various methodologies exist today for managing projects. The Agile method uses an iterative approach that allows rapid prototyping of a work product with the ability to gather feedback and make changes throughout the process, further refining and testing the product until completion. Waterfall methods use more linear sequencing of phases with less opportunity for changes throughout the project. Your choice of methods will vary greatly depending on your line of work; however, the ability to break down a large amount of work into smaller, manageable units is common to any successful project regardless of chosen methodology. This approach can be applied by students as well, from writing a research paper to tackling a group project.

Monitor Progress

Even the best plans face challenges and setbacks. The beauty of a plan can often be found in its ability to manage setbacks when they occur. Every plan must have contingency allowances that can be used specifically when something doesn't go as planned. In order to know when to use contingencies, we must first know when we have gone off course and be able to quickly identify delays or unexpected outcomes within any given task or phase. The earlier we become aware of these moments, the more quickly we can address a problem and take corrective action. This requires careful monitoring of progress among smaller units of work and determining if, at any point in time, the task is on target for the planned schedule. Whoever is planning the work—whether a project manager, supervisor, or workers themselves—must regularly assess progress against the plan and adjust future work accordingly. If a unit falls behind, what can be done to mitigate the delay: Add resources? Shorten the following phase? Reduce scope? Work overtime? Assessment on a regular basis allows us to refine the plan and make adjustments that allow the subsequent work to continue successfully.

Let's use the example of a software development project, shown in figure 11.2. For this example, I use a ninety-day period for product completion. The project, like other software development projects, consists of standard phases within a system development life cycle. There is no need to reinvent the wheel. I can use a basic plan similar to those used for other projects my team has completed.

Figure 11.2: Sample project outline

Week 1:	Conduct market research
Week 2:	Identify requirements
Weeks 3–5:	Develop detailed functional specifications
Weeks 6–9:	Write code and perform alpha testing
Week 10:	Resolve errors and perform acceptance test
Week 11:	Run final testing
Week 12:	Complete and deliver product

Having outlined a basic plan, I can start marking phases into the schedule and assigning smaller work tasks for the days or weeks in each phase, further refining each into smaller units of work. The schedule begins to take shape and can then be mapped out simply in a calendar app or more formally in project management software. Any future projects can also borrow from the basic plan and documented assessments of how well the plan worked, where setbacks occurred and why, and any mitigation steps taken. The plan can be further refined with more accurate estimations and insights as project knowledge accumulates over time. That plan can become a template for future project plans. Plan the work, then work the plan. This approach is useful for any scheduled work, and current technology can facilitate implementation and management of plans, allowing the work effort to support intended goals and objectives.

Phone and Tablets

Though smartphones are ubiquitous, their users commonly underutilize smartphone capabilities, with making calls, internet search, maps, and texting as the primary common uses. Similarly, with tablets, many users fail to recognize the full utility of these devices, citing entertainment and search as the most popular features. Both phones and tablets, however, have clever features and allow the installation of applications that we can use to improve our focus and management of priorities. Consider the following time-savers at your fingertips on your handheld device:

- ✓ voice recorder

- ✓ virtual sticky notes

- ✓ teleconference for virtual meetings

- ✓ camera (not just for photos but also screenshots, whiteboard notes, meeting flip charts, etc.)

- ✓ timer, stopwatch

- ✓ notifications

- ✓ distinctive ringtones

- ✓ night mode for sound suppression, dim backlight, and no interruptions

- ✓ Bluetooth for handsfree access and connection to other devices

- ✓ alarms and reminders

- ✓ calculator

✓ news feeds for current events, game scores, stock prices

✓ e-books

✓ voice activation for search, dial, text, dictation, and navigation

The voice recorder ability is great for recording things such as notes to self, meetings, and lectures. Recording questions for a colleague, a speech you are preparing, role-playing for an upcoming client interaction, or listening to your own presentation in your own voice can benefit any professional.

Videoconferencing is as easy as clicking on the video icon when making a call. Your caller can elect to answer with video or simply audio. While not necessary for all calls, it may be especially useful if you want to share a live view of something you are working on.

I use a memo app as I would a sticky note. When I think of something to add to my grocery list, hear a good book recommendation, or learn the name of a potential client or mentor, I can easily record it there.

The calendar feature makes your cloud-based schedule available anytime since nowadays most people always have their phone with them. Use it to enter appointments immediately when you schedule your next salon, doctor, or dentist visit. No lost appointment cards to worry about, and the cloud will sync it to your other devices. With the reminder feature on calendars, your phone can be set to chime a few minutes before an appointment and remind you to get ready to go. Alarms in the clock feature of your phone can be set to not only wake you in the morning but also to remind you when to transition to new tasks on your schedule. The timer and stopwatch features within the clock settings are useful when cooking, timing tasks, or counting down your break time.

Night mode is truly a gift. My days of being on-call 24/7 are long gone, and few things warrant waking me at 3 a.m. By setting night mode, I can ensure my good night's sleep is maintained without interruptions from telemarketers, wrong numbers, or a sleepless friend. Explore your phone's settings for ways to dim the backlight, reduce glare, eliminate sounds, and set times of day when you want silence.

Of course, having a camera built into the phone is great for photos, but it can also replace copying or scanning. In meetings, take a picture of the whiteboard and save yourself from having to take notes. Take a picture of flip charts, make a video of the demonstration, or capture a colleague's business card. Many phones' integrated cameras take much better photos than an office scanner. Try getting reference materials, journals, and books as e-books through an e-reader. Significantly lightening the load in your backpack, the phone becomes a portable virtual reference library. Having reading material on the phone comes in handy while waiting for the bus, a delayed connection, or while waiting in the school pickup line.

Direct email to your phone, and there is less need to open your computer to check email. Set up your purge settings so that the cloud removes old messages for you without having to manually review and delete.

One of my favorite phone features is voice activation (personal assistant). Advances in natural language processing have made this feature nearly foolproof. I use it profusely to dial calls, search on the internet, make dinner reservations, dictate documents, and create text messages. I love being able to simply speak into my phone and not have to type anything.

Many features in the phone can also minimize interruptions. One of the most obvious is caller ID. When your phone rings, caller ID shows the caller's name. You need not answer every call. There are quick text responses that can be selected when you choose to dismiss a call, informing the caller you are busy, will call them back, or choose from many other quick responses. Or you can simply not answer and dismiss the call with a tap on the screen or a swipe to the side. Voicemail is another interruption saver. An icon on your phone showing a voicemail exists doesn't mean you must listen to it right then. You choose when to listen to voice mails, maybe two to three times daily, and preserve your uninterrupted blocks of time.

Other interruptions from our phones come in the form of notifications. While a day trader may need to have stock price notices alert them immediately, most of us can decide when to check stock prices and not interrupt our work to do so. Same for sports scores and headlines. *You* decide when to check these; turn off notifications from those apps through the settings on your device. Constant alerts render the alert ineffective because too many alerts cause the brain to habituate and ignore them. It is like living near a train track—after a while you don't notice the train whistle. For notifications and alerts on the phone, minimize them to allow the important ones to truly alert you when necessary.

Bluetooth is indispensable while driving to enable us to drive with hands on the wheel and not on the phone, and it also shares music with the car speakers and connects to other devices wirelessly. Driving hands-free allows many business folks to utilize travel times as participants in meetings or in planning what to make for dinner on the way home. Creative use of technology allows us to make the most of our days without overburdening our already busy schedules.

My Favorite People

We all have those select few important callers whose calls we cannot ignore or defer. Our children, spouse, or boss may call, and we do not want to miss those calls. A great way to differentiate their calls is to assign each a distinctive ringtone. I have set them for my kids, my husband, my elderly parents, and some clients. My daughter's ringtone is a sweet melody; I've assigned the *Mission Impossible* theme to my son; my husband's calls blare our favorite song. I know immediately upon hearing those first few notes and without looking up from my work who is trying to reach me. And by designating them as favorites in my contacts settings, their calls can be the few allowed exceptions to my phone's silent mode. This is an extraordinarily handy feature, especially when you might be virtually unreachable during that important sales meeting when your spouse's flight got canceled and won't make it back to pick up the kids from school.

Many of us have to be reminded to silence our phones. Movie theatres, churches, and conferences routinely admonish patrons to silence devices as a courtesy to others. We can choose to silence our phones anytime we want to. It need not be buzzing or ringing all day long. Many occupations do not allow phones on the job—think of a surgeon or entertainer. Their work is done without any phone interruptions.

Aside from enabling a distinctive ringtone, we can also devise a special signal for our significant others and loved ones. Mine know that if it is an emergency and I do not pick up, they call back, let it ring once, and hang up, three times in a row. I know that signal is to pick up and answer immediately! This works even when they call from an unknown phone number, as an alternative to a distinctive ringtone notification.

Some features allow us to notify others in advance that we cannot or do not wish to be interrupted. Posting a status on social media or setting an email autoresponder can alert anyone trying to contact us that we are out of commission for the next few hours due to being in jury duty, taking an examination, traveling on an overseas flight, participating in an off-site training, or whatever you're doing that cannot be interrupted.

I am still learning about the many features available on my phone. And just when I become proficient, it is time for an upgrade, and I discover new capabilities to rock my world. We have certainly come a long way from those days of carrying a PalmPilot, flip phone, notebook, atlas, and nearly the entire contents of a desk within the briefcase just to conduct business on the road. Smartphones do it all.

Mission Control

Technology has transformed our lives in countless ways since the earliest days of computerization. Just as NASA's Apollo program mission control room in Houston was the epicenter for guiding the moon landing, the technology on our devices today is a trusted partner in supporting our greatest achievements. In your personal lunar landing, the mission control officer, however, is ultimately you. Only you can make the choices that propel you to great heights, ultimately with the power to enact or override even the smartest suggestions from Google and Siri. How and when we use the powerful tools of technology is up to us. Our intentions, values, goals, and aspirations are the pilots in the spaceship of life.

We can and should, however, take advantage of technology whenever possible to eliminate the mundane, address the repetitive, and simplify our lives. This leaves us more time to work toward our next great achievement and experience life to its fullest. As a lifelong proponent of computerization and technology, I've compiled a few final tips and technology features I find most helpful in keeping me on track and organized. Many of these are free tools already installed or available for download to your device.

✓ Keep your computer desktop tidy (with fewer than ten icons). Use folders wisely, and store your documents in folders that make sense. Poor organization skills are exacerbated by a messy computer desktop. Having hundreds of icons to choose from or finding a document misfiled upon download is maddening and stressful—a true sign that it is time to prioritize and focus.

✓ Use email rules to automatically file or respond to incoming messages without your intervention. This is a sorely underutilized capability that is a great time-saver. Some email apps have canned rules you can configure through settings, and some enable you to build your own rules with simple if-then statements or sophisticated code. This feature is the irreplaceable filing clerk of today.

✓ Use a virtual notes app or task list to integrate your thoughts with your calendar and email or to post to your computer screen as a visual reminder. Eliminate paper lists and notes on scraps of paper that can be easily lost and don't travel with you.

✓ Use headphones. Block out background noise and listen to calming sounds from nature or energizing music. Use audio to enhance your productivity and improve your mood.

✓ Back up your device to the cloud. Set up a schedule to back up content regularly to prevent loss and allow portability of your important content across devices. Many apps are available for limited amounts of free cloud storage. Invest in paid storage, if necessary, to hold everything you need. There is no worse avoidable time waster than having to redo work because it was not backed up. Unfortunately, scheduled backup of data is something most computer users do not really think about until they lose something they need. Most services allow real-time backup so your files are safe immediately. Once you set it up, you will never have to think about it again. Cloud storage of documents allows all your devices to remain synchronized, and no matter where you enter content, cloud storage keeps everything current.

A Parting Thought

Whenever I hear the phrase *managing time*, I am reminded of the arcade game Whac-a-Mole. Metaphorically, as a time "mole" pops its head up from the hole, we must quickly beat it down, reacting with reflexes. *Fighting fires* is a common analogy used in the workplace for dealing with sudden urgent demands. This is no way to live and work (unless, of course, you are a firefighter). Imagine, instead, strolling down the yellow brick road—a path laid out, brick by brick, to guide us on our journey to our own Oz. When we learn to view time as *experienced* rather than *spent*, Oz becomes viewable on the horizon and can be reached after an exciting and deliberate trek. How we think about time has considerable impact on how we experience time. If we are lucky, we may even experience adventures and unexpected joy along the way.

PART FOUR
RESILIENCE: LEARNING TO THRIVE

CHAPTER 12
Moving the Dial Toward Thriving

Toddlers are fascinating to watch. They exhibit more energy and enthusiasm than any Super Bowl cheer squad I've ever seen. They seem to have an endless zest for life and can't wait to soak up all the world has to offer, exuding unbridled joy and wonder. Once they are walking and then talking, they are often said to be thriving as they learn new skills at an extraordinary pace, acquire knowledge of their world, and enjoy a newfound freedom of mobility and communication. And, as toddlers, they experience countless spills, bumps and bruises, crying fits, and the like. Yet they pick themselves up (or are picked up by a loving parent) and start right back in on adventures after momentary fits of despair. They bounce back remarkably. They are resilient, never letting a skinned knee or goose egg on the forehead keep them from whatever comes next. Their zeal remains, for many, throughout childhood but slowly diminishes to a point of near extinction by the time they reach puberty. By adulthood, these emotions and behaviors become fossils from our distant past. Why is this so?

The thriving toddler plays, explores, and experiences every situation with a ready awareness, a budding curiosity, and boundless opportunities for growth. By adulthood, especially in Western cultures, we seem to lose those abilities or fail to exercise them on a regular basis. But as adults, we can rediscover and exercise deliberate behaviors that allow us to reap more satisfaction from life and work and help ourselves begin to flourish and thrive throughout adult life with the vigor and awe of our toddler selves. We can become kids at heart. We can coach ourselves and train our brains to rekindle those experiences. We can enhance our work, relationships, and personal life. We can help ourselves bounce back from the numerous setbacks, challenges, and hardships common in adult life. We can use techniques from the latest research in neuroscience, positive psychology, wellness, and cognitive psychology to jump-start our stalling engines and get back on the road.

Languish or Flourish?

The work of positive psychology researchers contributes much to our understanding of optimal human functioning and flourishing. We can either allow ourselves to languish or instead learn to flourish despite the current state of affairs in life. Think of sunflowers in a field in July, reaching toward the sun, getting full and lush with verdant leaves. They are flourishing. Think, also, of that same field in mid-September, after a particularly arid summer. Leaves are a dull green, flower heads droop with curled petals, and stems are shriveling. They are languishing—alive but just hanging on. They could be better (with water and sun). And by autumn they have withered, turned brown, and gone to seed, devoid of life. We, as do sunflowers, thrive in the right conditions, droop in poor conditions, and become sick or die when disease sets in or when sustenance subsides. This chapter is dedicated to creating the right conditions that allow us to thrive, flourish, and foster resilience despite tough times.

Let's ask ourselves a few questions to determine our current flourish rating. Think about your current outlook on life right now and how positive and happy you feel. You can rate yourself using the informal scale in figure 12.1.

Figure 12.1: Flourish rating scale

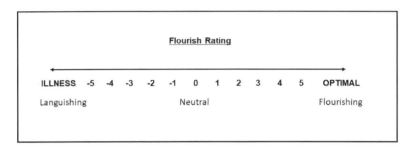

Ask yourself the following questions:

- *Are you upbeat and thriving?*

- *Are you the best you can be?*

If you answered yes to one of these questions, you'd likely fall somewhere on the right side of the scale. If you answered yes to both, you are likely near the far-right side, near the point of flourishing. On the other hand, consider these questions:

- *Are you just managing to get by every day?*

- *Are you working on autopilot?*

- *Are you simply surviving?*

- *Are you just okay, neither bad nor great?*

A yes answer to one or more of these should land you somewhere around zero, close to the point of languishing, or the neutral point. Finally, answer these questions:

- *Are you on the decline?*

- *Are you extremely unhappy or in distress?*

If you answered yes to either of these two questions, you'd be more at the left end of the scale, possibly dealing with illness or experiencing hardship.

The flourish rating is subjective; it is just for your own use. Don't dwell on it; simply go with your gut reaction. As always, we start with awareness. Being aware of our current outlook gives a starting point from which to measure progress as we learn to flourish.

If your flourish rating in this informal exercise was a 4 or above, congratulations and keep up whatever you're doing. Chances are you're already using some of the techniques of flourishing. Few people honestly report a 5. Even so, we can all do more to thrive and become more positive and satisfied and develop into our better selves. If you are at −1, 0, or a low positive number, I hope to inspire you to learn and practice your flourishing skills. If you are at the extreme left end of the scale, I encourage you to seek professional counseling and also learn and practice the flourishing skills presented in this book.

As a coach, I work with clients who want more from themselves, who want to do more, be more, experience more, overcome challenges, realize their potential, and succeed in their work, life, and relationships. I share with them the evidence-based, research-driven practices that anyone can learn that will help them grow and improve their lives. In doing so, they are better equipped to flourish and experience abundance and true well-being! Practicing these techniques can produce measurable outcomes as demonstrated by a growing amount of research in positive psychology, neuroscience, cognition, and human emotion.

Look at the definition of these two words in figure 12.2: *languish* and *flourish*.

Figure 12.2: Definitions of languish and flourish

Languish	Flourish
to become weak or feeble; fade	to exist in a vigorous state; thrive
to lose vigor and vitality	to be successful; prosper
to experience prolonged inactivity	to grow luxuriantly
to suffer hardship and distress	to experience abundant growth (be happy?)

To *languish* is to be more like the sunflower that has passed or never reached its prime; to *flourish* is to be more like the vibrant sunflower reaching toward the sun. Wouldn't you rather be flourishing?

What does it mean to be happy? The answer is as individual as each one of us. Positive psychologists study happiness and factors that contribute to our overall outlook on life.[20] They contend that only about 50 percent of our happiness and outlook on life can be attributed to our genes, predestined by way of heredity. That is, if our parents are pessimists, we may inherent a predisposition toward pessimism, but it only accounts for part of our view of the world. Life circumstances account for another 10 percent. Living in poverty or wealth, in a large or small family, city or rural area, for example, has even less impact than genetics. Once our basic physical needs are met, our genetics are accounted for, and we have sufficient means to survive in the world, there is still a large percentage left for us to develop our own potential for happiness—up to 40 percent! Many of these studies utilize identical twins who were raised apart as subjects in determining the influence of heredity and life circumstances. Twins living apart in varied social and economic circumstances help illuminate the impact heredity has on our outlook. This line of research generated the conclusion that a large portion of happiness and life outlook is within our control, despite heredity and environment. How content we are, how fully we realize our potential, how easily we recover from setbacks and hardship, and our overall attitude depends largely on how we think and behave.

Within ourselves, we have the power to move that dial to the right, maybe moving from a +2 to a +5 on the informal flourishing scale in figure 12.1. We can unleash the power to go from good to great—not just to avoid depression or illness or get back to net zero but rather to move toward a more positive, optimal human experience. There is a big difference between the absence of depression, illness, or negativity (languishing) and actively flourishing or thriving. The absence of disease does not mean good health. Not bad is just that—it is not great. We can strive for great, and in doing so, we can position ourselves to experience the abundant growth and resilience of a field of sunflowers.

There are common behaviors among those people who flourish:

✓ aspire

✓ live with purpose and direction

✓ look forward

✓ keep an open mind

✓ express gratitude

✓ bounce back

✓ have good things come their way

✓ see opportunities where others see challenges

When I was a child, my mother loved watching the movie *Singin' in the Rain*.[21] There was a memorable scene in which Gene Kelly danced and splashed around in puddles, singing in the rain. That scene and its catchy song remind me of how someone who is flourishing might feel inside.

You might argue that it is easy to sing and dance, or flourish, when everything is going well. Yet there are countless instances of people living in deplorable, often dangerous and dire, circumstances who have suffered unimaginable pain and feel happy. We all know of someone who has survived tragedy and yet manages to not only recover from it but thrive. It is a fallacy that people can flourish and be happy only because nothing bad has happened to them. When bad things happen to those who flourish, they bounce back more quickly. They are *resilient*. They see opportunities where others see challenges. They are the proverbial makers of lemonade, looking for silver linings. Challenges, hardship, and pain do not preclude flourishing. Flourishing involves behaviors and thought patterns that can be learned, and those who flourish have mastered and continue to develop these behaviors and ways of thinking. They take control of their experiences and rise above or transcend despite bad experiences. Research shows that flourishing can help buffer the effects of life's hardships and creates resilience. People who flourish are on a journey: They work at it, believe in it, and persist. They look forward. They feel as if they are moving toward something, not treading water or biding time. Science tells us that actively thinking and behaving like people who flourish has lasting impact.

The Science of Well-Being

Before about thirty years ago, researchers in the field of psychology studied negative emotions: anger, fear, depression, aggression, and anxiety. The field evolved to where cognitive and social psychologists as well as behavioral economists started studying decision-making, attitudes, and behaviors in the absence of illness or negative emotion.[22] Some of the world's most prominent researchers began looking at emotion, optimal human experience, and what makes people well.[23] There are many who have contributed to the science of well-being and positive psychology, and exciting advances in neuroscience and fascinating new brain imaging techniques, like the functional MRI, have propelled the research forward and discovered major breakthroughs.[24]

World-class researchers and thousands of empirical studies in medical, psychology, and business journals have contributed to the science of well-being—yes, the *science* of well-being. There is considerable rigor in these peer-reviewed studies, and as theories start to converge, we see facts emerging, the building of a paradigm. Positive psychology is relatively new to the broader field of psychology, with most research occurring within the last twenty years. When I studied psychology as an undergrad in the early 1980s and later as a graduate student, much of the focus was on the negative emotions such as fear, anger, and prejudice. There had been a strong emphasis on disease and mental illness, while subsequent research from social and cognitive psychology and behavioral economics contributed to the beginning of positive psychology and the science of wellness or well-being.

What is meant by the *science* of well-being? Researchers are trying to understand what causes us to feel happy, satisfied, less stressed, connected, and motivated. The theories are tested empirically, statistically validated, and replicated in various populations and situations to yield predictive and reliable results. The findings can be applied to family life, work, relationships, and business due to their replication across situations, cultures, and different populations. In coaching, I teach my clients about these findings so they can incorporate the techniques into their everyday life and work—techniques that can be practiced and mastered and, when applied on an ongoing basis, enable personal transformation.

Practical Techniques for Flourishing

Several major contributors and theories laid the foundation for flourishing techniques and their role in improving your well-being. And by doing a few exercises, you will get a chance to think about your own life situation and generate some ideas around how flourishing might apply to you.

Daniel Kahneman is also known for his work in decision-making.

His decades of research on memory and human experience developed many principles on which positive psychology and well-being are built. He studied how people think about their various life experiences, especially negative ones, and the role of memory in experience.[25] He has contributed to our understanding of how people think, our natural tendencies, the heuristics our brains use, and particularly errors in judgment. His research shows us that an experience is subjective and can be viewed entirely differently by two different people, and more importantly, he suggests how we can control our interpretation of an experience. And the idea of *interpretation of experience* is a key component of well-being. Much of this work has become a springboard for positive psychology, lead to the development of cognitive therapy for mental health, and inspired a tremendous amount of research in neuroscience, behavioral economics, and positive psychology and wellness.

The research on cognitive bias helps us understand the basic thought processes in the brain and our natural responses. With this awareness, we can begin to mitigate these and *choose* more thoughtful behavior and responses. This research is being applied today by tech companies aiming to develop more functional apps, user interfaces, websites, and more recently in applications of artificial intelligence.[26]

Many of the known cognitive biases and natural thought tendencies become barriers to our well-being unless we learn to mitigate them. The mitigation involves two components. The first is being aware of our brain's natural tendencies as we experience a situation. Bringing awareness to our own thought patterns requires some practice. We need to take notice and reflect on what we are thinking while having the thoughts. The second component involves choosing how to react, think, or behave while acknowledging our natural tendencies and consciously redirecting our responses accordingly. Understanding these biases is crucial to overcoming them.

Here are some of the barriers to well-being:

- ✗ negativity bias

- ✗ duration neglect

- ✗ social comparison

- ✗ hedonic treadmill

- ✗ impulsivity

As in communications, the *negativity bias* has us dwell on the negativity we hear, experience, and feel. For wellness, we must work diligently to overcome this bias so negative thoughts do not rule us and our behavior. In human evolution, survival depended on the ability to remember and detect physical threats in the environment, such as the sudden approach of a bear or lion. We could argue there is less need for such vigilance today. Once adaptive in evolution, nowadays we don't contend with physical survival challenges that plagued our early human ancestors, and a focus on negativity and threats today is maladaptive to the point that it precludes our focus on more positive experiences and more adaptive behavior.

Other cognitive biases detract from our ability to flourish. *Duration neglect* (see chapter 8) is our brain's interpretation of an event based on the intensity and ending of the experience, regardless of how long it lasted. One application of this is to do something good for yourself at the end of a bad day. Duration bias will facilitate well-being despite the preceding negative experiences.

Social comparison is our tendency to compare ourselves and our lives to that of others—in other words, "keeping up with the Jones." To address this bias, gratitude is a useful counter measure. We can call to mind those less fortunate and elicit a sense of gratitude for our own good fortune. Or we can avoid extensive use of social media, known for its broadcasting of all the great things others are doing. Some of my clients suffering from poor self-esteem decided for themselves to get off of social media, turn off notifications, or temporarily unplug to reduce bombardment from social media braggarts. Researchers have begun to look at the negative effects of social media particularly in regard to social comparison and depression.[27] In coaching, we emphasize the client's progress and articulation of his or her own goals without reference to others' accomplishments and experiences to keep the focus on one's own well-being and goals and avoid the tendency to measure against others. By encouraging clients to set their own measures of success and progress and to help them recognize and celebrate their own successes along the way, we minimize attention to others' activities and encourage self-worth to grow. This practice can overcome the social comparison bias. Clearly articulating your own goals and setting metrics meaningful to you, and perhaps creating visual reminders of these to keep you focused on them, will counteract the potentially harmful comparisons sparked by others' online posts.

A considerable threat to flourishing is the *hedonic treadmill* bias, the adaptation effect we experience when we get used to something and the novelty wears off. Much like the effects of tolerance in substance abuse, when you continue doing something that makes you feel good, eventually those good feelings fade, and more and more is required to get you back to that level. One technique used to combat the treadmill effect is to *savor*, a means of keeping positive experiences in mind and providing residual pleasure. Like receiving dividends from a great investment, savoring allows us to experience positive emotion from reliving a happy time from our past through remembering, thinking about, and talking about it. Examples of savoring include creating a photo album of your recent trip, posting photos on your Pinterest board, talking about it online with others or to revisit yourself, creating a scrapbook, writing a journal entry or blog about an experience, placing a photo frame on your desk, or simply telling others about your experience. For those who use relaxation techniques, revisiting a special time in your mind with visual and sensory imagery can invoke the same positive experiences over and over again. Relaxation techniques using the recall of all five sensations—vision, smell, taste, touch, hearing—are particularly effective in savoring a positive experience.

Impulsivity, or poor self-regulation, is another primitive brain artifact from Neanderthal times that works against flourishing by thwarting our efforts to achieve goals. Impulsive behavior is when we act without thinking, giving little or no thought to consequences. The prefrontal cortex area of the brain is considered instrumental in regulating impulsivity. Several disease states and mental health disorders impact impulsivity and our decision-making abilities. Impulsivity is often associated with negative results, risk-taking behaviors, inability to focus attention, emotional reaction, and impatience. It often places more value on short-term rewards than long-term goals. It derails our intentions for positive behavior. We must work at channeling our efforts purposefully to avoid negative impulses that work against our real goals. Use of reminders stating your goals, rewarding yourself for remaining disciplined, setting incremental milestones to regulate and guide your immediate tasks are all ways to self-regulate and reject impulsive tendencies. Understanding these tendencies positions us to take control and rein in our thoughts and actions to support flourishing behaviors. We can learn to overcome these natural tendencies through awareness and practice, otherwise they become barriers to our well-being.

By recognizing barriers in our ability to flourish, we can devise ways to reduce or eliminate them. We can equip ourselves with psychological and behavioral tools that build our reserves and combat the pervasive tendency to languish.

CHAPTER 13
Flowing Down the River of Human Performance

The fields of wellness and positive psychology also developed through the study of optimal human functioning. Some examined what enables people to lose themselves in their work, art, writing, and other activities that virtually consume the mind and foster prolific work. MIT researcher Mihaly Csikszentmihalyi defined the state of consciousness called *flow* as a state of optimal human experience.[28] He studied those who do things for the sheer joy of it—dancers, artists, inventors, chess players—and identified a set of common characteristics of experiencing flow:

- ✓ is "in the zone"

- ✓ is totally engaged

- ✓ has a balance of challenge and skill

- ✓ has clear goals with prompt feedback

- ✓ gets totally immersed in the activity

- ✓ feels at one with the task

- ✓ is not concerned about failing

- ✓ loses track of time

✓ doesn't feel self-conscious

✓ wants to do it

In examining the flow state, Csikszentmihalyi learned how people behave and think when they are fully engaged in doing something they love and when experiencing an inherent satisfaction unmatched by other behaviors. It seems the flow state offers the ideal human experience and understanding. Flow provides insight as to how people can become more satisfied, productive, and happy. Interestingly, he found that the flow state can occur with everyday or mundane activities as well as work; some people reported flow states while housecleaning, mowing the lawn, doing chores, or playing with children.

A key component of flow is that the task and one's ability are well matched, yet there is some challenge. Boring, easy tasks do not elicit the state of flow (unless a degree of challenge is introduced, such as doing it faster). The activity must have clear goals and require skills one has already obtained, with just enough challenge to make it interesting but not seemingly impossible. People in flow state describe their experiences in much the same way, regardless of the activity. They are in the zone, completely absorbed in their own little world. They do not feel forced into it. They lose track of time, even forego breaks, meals, or sleep. They feel confident in their abilities and do not worry about failing or what may others think. They are not self-conscious. And they *want* to do it.

Yet the activities that generate a flow state are as individual as each of us. We each have our own interests that elicit flow, but few of us think about it in such terms. For example, creating a great design on the lawn while mowing could create just enough challenge to ramp up this seemingly dull activity and enable a flow state to occur. Some may find flow while solving a difficult problem, like working through a math proof, crafting the perfect novel, or playing a violin concerto.

In coaching clients, one exercise I use is to have the client identify when they have ever been in a flow state. We look at as many examples as they can muster and then start to examine if they are doing those activities currently, how often, and when it may have stopped. In order to flourish, we need to build regular flow time into our everyday lives. It may not be something you are able to fit in every day, but it should be frequent enough to give you the benefits that flow imparts—mastery over your environment, freedom from judgment, positive emotion, and more. Some people aim for flow in their job. Some people cannot find flow in their job but experience flow in a hobby they do after hours, letting the job be a way to indulge that hobby. The job is viewed as a means for providing financial independence and freedom to pursue the hobby and other building behaviors. If experiencing flow at work, we must be careful not to let the pressure in a job work against it. Deadlines and extrinsic goals will quickly squash flow.

During coaching sessions, we examine many possibilities for flow with the intent to have the client build more opportunity for flow experiences into their world. Some people rediscover old or identify new interests or invest more time in current pastimes that could elicit this state. In doing so, they are able to build their reserves and fortify their resilience tool kit, better enabling themselves to withstand challenges and hardships when they occur. You, too, can consider what brings you flow and regularly incorporate opportunities into your life, enabling optimal functioning.

Flow allows a respite from those tasks that create a weary mind. It frees up the mind for creativity and problem-solving. It enables us to experience the autonomy and competency so vital to our psychological health. We may feel ecstatic, get sudden clarity, or experience timelessness. Flow restores our reserves and builds resiliency, which helps protect us when tough times hit. It is when we are at peak performance. Striving for an increased frequency of flow in our lives has lasting effects. It causes dramatic changes in the brain as demonstrated in EEGs (electroencephalograms) and fMRIs (functional magnetic resonance imaging). The brain waves change from beta (fast and spiked) to smoother, steady alpha waves, reducing neural clutter from distractions and allowing deep concentration. There is an increase in the release of neurotransmitters (brain chemicals) that facilitate peak performance and sharpen our abilities: dopamine, the pleasure producer; norepinephrine, the energizer and sensory sharpener; serotonin, the wakefulness gatekeeper; and endorphins, euphoria generators. In addition, flow is associated with an increased level of anandamide, a naturally occurring opiate involved in the generation of new cells. The beneficial result of invoking internal mechanisms for peak performance is unmistakable and worth working toward and contributes to our well-being through natural brain processes.

The PERMA Theory

In the early 1980s, positive psychologist Martin Seligman was known for his prolific work on depression, including his theory of learned helplessness. Since then, however, Seligman turned his focus away from mental illness and toward the science of wellness and well-being. He is considered by some as the father of positive psychology. His PERMA theory identifies five major determinants and factors of well-being and the "good life," or what he calls *flourishing*. Seligman emphasizes that well-being and flourishing involve a set of behaviors that are both measurable and teachable, and he recommends leveraging individual strengths to develop these five areas more fully: positive emotion, engagement, relationships, meaning, and achievement.

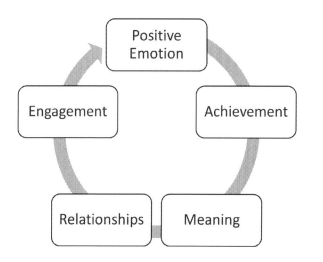

Figure 13.1: Seligman's PERMA components

According to Seligman, each of the five elements are necessary to attain well-being.[29] *Positive emotion* in PERMA can be described as enjoyment. *Engagement* is the feeling of being willingly involved and invested in a regular activity (work, hobbies, community service), much like the idea of Csikszentmihalyi's flow. The importance of *relationships,* much like relatedness in Richard Ryan's basic psychological needs in chapter 2, is another component of PERMA so critical to well-being. Relationships with family, loved ones, friends, or community members or even simple greetings with others can provide this component. Human connection, not simply being part of a crowd of strangers, is crucial to PERMA. PERMA also introduces the idea of *meaning* as a determinant of well-being. Purposeful and meaningful participation in life, through a feeling of a higher purpose, influences our ability to thrive. Purpose may be attained through religion, community, politics, or family and may involve a sense of belonging. The last of the five PERMA factors is *achievement,* or accomplishment. Seligman places emphasis on individuals' feelings of success and competence. In order to experience well-being, we must have mastery over our environment. All five factors can be measured.

In coaching, I examine these five areas for a holistic view of each client. Clients identify what actions they engage in that support each of the five factors of PERMA. We articulate example behaviors for each, quantitatively defining each element with the client's current activity. If there are factors that have relatively few occurrences compared to the others, we determine if those are areas the client wants to develop. We then identify which of the client's strengths can be used to further build that factor. What is so critical to this theory is that the factors can be measured, quantified, and developed. With or without a coach, these elements can be identified and cultivated by an individual through deliberate behavior.

In 2012, the US military spent $145 million teaching PERMA and resilience to soldiers. As part of the Comprehensive Soldier

Fitness program, Seligman's teachings were used to enhance psychological resilience and better enable psychologically healthy military personnel to overcome the stress of combat and family separation. In the United Kingdom, former Prime Minister David Cameron developed a comprehensive wellness policy and began measuring well-being in his country. In Adelaide, South Australia, leaders implemented a project in the public school system to teach positive emotion and resilience to students. World leaders and corporations are recognizing the valuable scientific contributions in the field of well-being and are beginning to create programs to inspire growth.

Asian and European countries have adopted coaching as a means of educating individuals and organizations on the science of applied positive psychology. Fortune 500 companies are embarking on wellness programs to combat burnout and foster employee health. In the United States, however, we are lagging in the practical application of wellness science, although our research contributions are great. Coaching, leadership training, and therapy are increasingly using the principles from well-being science. There remains a great opportunity for applying these practices even earlier in life to equip youth with these important skills for self-care and growth. Adolescents especially could benefit from learning techniques of flourishing, becoming more resilient and protected against the common struggles of puberty. If learned early, teens could further hone these skills well before adulthood, better positioning them for success and satisfaction in school and later in life.

I've coached college students and young adults who benefit from exploring the facets of PERMA. So focused on accomplishments and engagement while working toward a degree or entering the job market, this population often neglects several other areas of PERMA.

Amelia, a stellar student with aspirations for medical school, found herself increasingly unmotivated and dissatisfied with her current undergraduate life. She had excellent grades, received academic recognition, and was awarded monetary and scholarly commendations, but she found her social life waning. Amelia noticed she was spending less time on her interests outside of school, and she had started to question her decision to apply to medical school. She was starting to feel burnt out and asked herself, "After all, what's it all for?"

In the coaching process, we considered what she was doing in each area of PERMA. Amelia realized she had withdrawn from the musical group she had been part of, and her flute sat in the corner of her dorm gathering dust. She missed the camaraderie of the quintet and interacting with the other musicians. She realized how much playing the flute meant to her, the feeling of total immersion she felt while playing a challenging piece (flow!). Especially interesting was her realization that after rehearsing and playing a gig with the quintet she felt a renewed interest in her studies and became energized to tackle the next round of work. The quintet, it seems, had satisfied not only engagement for her but also provided Amelia with relationships and a sense of accomplishment. It offered positive emotion and opportunities for flow and buffered her from burnout. Amelia eventually worked out time in her schedule to resume her flute practice and started playing with the quintet again.

At first it meant practicing the flute for fifteen minutes every other day or so. Then, the amount of time and number of days spent practicing increased as she became more absorbed in the music (flow) and found herself rejuvenated after a practice session. She learned that by doing so, she experienced many positive emotions from within herself and through others. She gave herself a well-deserved and frequent respite from serious study and concentrated work, renewing her interest in pursuing her academic goals. Music *builds* Amelia. In exploring and committing to what it is that builds us, we are better able to combat burnout and stress and overcome tough times. What builds us is what sustains us.

There are some key observations from the research on well-being. Positivity is only partially attributed to heredity and life circumstances. There is a range of happiness versus depression or optimism versus pessimism that we are born with, and life circumstances also impact our ability to experience happiness. Notably, the remainder is to a great extent within our control. We can push the needle to the right on the flourish scale, moving from a +2 to a +4 or from 0 to +3; we can move toward the high end of the spectrum with a little training and practice. We can go from good to great, from ho-hum to happier, by developing our skills that build. Our happiness is more about *doing* and less about *being*. That is why we (especially young people) must learn skills, informed by the well-being science, that build us and protect us in challenging times. Resilience enables us to bear hardship and overcome seemingly insurmountable challenges and come out on the other side with a forward-thinking mindset. It propels us past the horrific and toward hope. It allows us to grow and flourish. By intentionally choosing how we spend our time and how we behave, we build our internal resources and facilitate our own well-being.

Basic Psychological Needs Impact Performance

As reviewed in chapter 2, the basic psychological needs theory (BPNT) contends that a failure to meet basic psychological needs not only inhibits psychological health but also our ability to function optimally within our environment.[30] Just as relatedness boosts our psychological well-being, optimal functioning is also contingent on autonomy and competence. Failure to meet these important psychological needs (see figure 13.2) results in a lack of thriving. Note the similarities between BPNT and PERMA. The satisfaction of these needs impacts our motivation and ability to flourish and function optimally in our world. If we are struggling to meet our basic needs, we become less motivated to thrive.

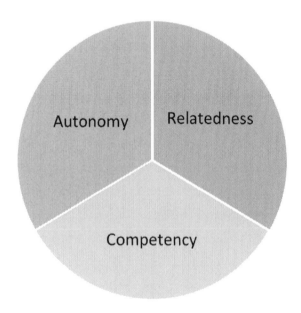

Figure 13.2: Basic psychological needs theory

Communications with others satisfies a basic psychological need for relatedness. Solitary living or isolation hinders the satisfaction of this need. By effectively communicating with others, we improve our well-being and optimal functioning as people in communities and in the workplace.

Interestingly, *relatedness* is universally rated as one of the most important values, yet it is often one of the most neglected aspects in the workplace, schools, and clinical environments. The COVID-19 pandemic's impact on remote work adversely affected the ability to satisfy the relatedness need for many. It has become ever more crucial to create new opportunities for connecting with others in novel ways.

Relatedness can be promoted in the workplace, and this was an important aspect of one of my corporate coaching engagements. My client was part of the leadership team of a large health system with hospitals and administrative offices across several states, in some instances thousands of miles apart. One of the organization's strategic goals was to integrate leadership and foster a cohesive and unified experience for patients and employees across the health system, despite disparate state and local practices, policy differences, multiple medical specialties, and unique administrative styles. Using technology to facilitate connection among the leaders, the organization implemented a videoconferencing platform that enabled leaders to convene in meetings with their distant counterparts virtually sitting across the table from them. The platform, through a file share and room-size video monitor, enabled a group seated at a large boardroom oval table in one state to appear on the other group's monitor, virtually completing the other side of the oval table. Charts, documents, and presentations were displayed for each site simultaneously, while viewing their colleagues seated in the distant boardroom. It essentially allowed the oval table to become intact.

Discussions became much more interactive, facial expressions and body language could also be considered with a more natural back-and-forth exchange of ideas. As a whole the group reported feeling more connected to each other than through voice conferencing alone. While this was a large technology investment, in doing so the organization underscored their goal of integrating leadership and connecting distant colleagues with the benefits inherent in connected communications. And travel costs were reduced as a by-product of the reduction in on-site meetings. It differed from other videoconferencing in its ability to show a room full of people in a singular view from the perspective of one sitting across the table.

Workplaces using Agile methodology, where team members, virtually or in-person, check in daily with each other for a brief ten-minute "stand-up" meeting, or those using regular "huddles" popular in continuous improvement initiatives have also employed videoconferencing to foster inclusiveness among remote team members and those on-site. Perhaps unaware of the science behind relatedness, these teams realize the benefits and importance of the connections for team effectiveness. It satisfies a basic psychological need and fosters relatedness at work.

In conducting workshops, I meet and hear from many business owners, contractors, and freelancers who in the absence of a traditional workplace lament a loss of relatedness. Countless networking groups and professional organizations serve a crucial need for social interaction for these nontraditional workers. And with the rise of coworking spaces, lone practitioners, freelancers, and entrepreneurs have more opportunity to find relatedness at work, even if their workplace is a company of one.

Autonomy, another factor in the basic psychological needs theory, is the desire to make decisions for one's self. Using volition and initiative, we make choices on what to do, how to do it, and when. Children gradually become more autonomous as they grow, and allowing children an age-appropriate autonomy is part of a healthy childhood. Autonomy is, however, one aspect of motivation often suppressed in work environments, particularly in lower-paying jobs. Yet people in the most seemingly mundane jobs and work environments can bring a sense of autonomy to their work by introducing novelty or utilizing their strengths, thereby creating a more enjoyable and positive work experience for themselves.

Some professionals enjoy the luxury of setting their own schedule, work hours, and even what type of work they will do. Those working in minimum-wage jobs, on assembly lines, in factories, or in the service industries typically have a more rigid work environment with much less flexibility. They too, however, can exercise autonomy in creative ways within their workday or on breaks. They can decide how to spend their breaks and lunch, choose to vary the route to and from work, and determine whom they interact with and how. They might set goals for themselves in terms of productivity within a given time frame (a beat-the-clock scenario), set out to learn another job within the company, or develop a unique approach to perform their job. With a bit of creativity, even the most tedious work situation can be made more interesting through choices you make for yourself.

This often comes up during coaching when a client is bored with their job. We evaluate opportunities for choices that could liven things up and make the job more interesting. We explore options for change and ways to introduce a degree of autonomy in a seemingly dull work scenario. I ask, "What choices have you made for yourself today?" Often clients have difficulty identifying when they do exercise their own volition. One employee in a retail operation set out to learn each regular customer's name and product preferences so she could greet them and anticipate their needs when they walked into the store. This became an enjoyable challenge that made the sometimes-dull job more interesting and fun.

Bored workers present an interesting coaching challenge. We look at what it is that tires them, brainstorm alternative choices they would and could make, and identify any barriers to exercising those choices. This is a retrospection anyone can do without a coach. One trick is to uncover what is within one's control, discovering choices that have been made and are perhaps unrecognized, where these choices *are* possible, and the barriers that exist, real or perceived.

The third component of the basic psychological needs theory is *competency*. The ability to develop and perform with skill and leverage our individual strengths is important for psychological health. We derive satisfaction from using our skills and completing work. We all know the satisfaction of doing something well. Whether it is landing that new client, writing a cogent article, acing an exam, perfecting a soufflé, or improving our own personal record in a 5k race, a job well done is satisfying! The key here is your individual definition of a job well done. My 5k jog at an 8:44 pace may be way too slow for you, but if I were to beat it, I'd be thrilled. My goal is to improve my performance and enjoy the rewards of my training and persistence. This holds true at work too. My pace of climbing the career ladder may not match yours. So what? It is our ability to define success *for ourselves* that matters. We need to be able to exercise competency in some areas of our personal and professional lives. It allows the flow state to be possible. Competence is what inspires children to learn new ways of interacting in the world. Competence breeds more competence. It spirals into burgeoning achievement.

A corollary to experiencing competence is that we must recognize and celebrate those achievements—large and small. We can learn to savor those moments for residual feelings of well-being. By doing this, we can call up those same feelings, the positive emotions, generated during the original event time and time again. The recognition and celebration need not be from others. We can and should acknowledge and embrace our own achievements. Too often, we overlook just what we have accomplished and how far we have progressed on our journey.

Richard Ryan's competence factor is also one that can be cultivated. We can identify those skills or talents we want to develop and set out to improve them through training, reading, and practice. Note that all three factors of BPNT are not static entities. The factors ebb and flow throughout our lives. It is up to us to recognize and periodically assess how well we are doing in addressing the three at a given point in time and take action to achieve more balance among them when the scales tip low in an area.

Since our life goals, motivation, and personal happiness are enabled by having met the basic needs, an imbalance or a perceived imbalance must be corrected. One challenge in coaching is to facilitate clients' recognition of their own behaviors and acknowledgment of choices they *do* make or *could* make for themselves. We do ourselves a great disservice if we fail to take stock on how we fare in terms of the three basic psychological needs because unmet needs result in a diminished ability to thrive. So in developing a wellness strategy, we strive to incorporate more behaviors and activities into our everyday lives to meet these needs, thereby cultivating growth in each area and better positioning ourselves to thrive. My coaching clients often have some difficulty articulating when they are exercising choice and how they are meeting basic needs, and we bring awareness to how they think about choices and decisions they have made. Take these clients for example:

- *Autonomy*—Tyra has a rather mundane and repetitive job. There is not much flexibility in what she must do and how it is done since she must follow protocol. However, Tyra does have a choice in what hours to work. So one way she satisfies the need for autonomy is by choosing to work seven in the morning to three in the afternoon to minimize her commuting time.

- *Competency*—In his college days, Matt played on the school's NCAA basketball team. He once excelled at it and considered a professional sports career. Though Matt works in banking now, during his off-hours he coaches a youth league and uses his skills on the court to develop young players.

As an exercise, you can examine your own behaviors and assess how well you are developing in the three basic psychological needs. What are you doing to feel related, autonomous, and competent? To lay the foundation for resilience and thriving, we must actively work to satisfy the three basic psychological needs and recognize those choices we do make for ourselves that can positively or negatively impact the satisfaction of those needs.

Flow Exercise

Because of its natural ability to restore well-being, it is important to first identify the activities that elicit flow in us, then cultivate opportunities to incorporate flow into our lives with regularity. This exercise will help you determine when and how often you experience flow, plan ways to regularly introduce flow into your schedule, and reinforce its practice through reflection on the benefits you feel after a flow state.

1. Consider all the activities you have done over the past week—such as work, hobbies, family time, socializing, chores, or volunteering. It may help to look at your calendar to help remember what occurred over the last seven days.

2. List those that give you a flow experience. (You may discover some surprises and unexpected flow states!) Include any degree of flow—whether it lasted for ten minutes or ten hours. The important thing is to think about your experience: Was it enjoyable? Were you immersed? Was it at least somewhat challenging? Were your skills enough? Was it your choice to engage? Did you lose track of time?

3. If you had no flow state over the past week, look further back into the past until you can identify at least two times.

4. Identify time this week for when you will do some of those flow activities again. Update your calendar to reflect time set aside for flow activity. Commit to doing it at least twice a

week initially for twenty minutes or more; work up to greater frequency and duration in the next month.

5. After the next time you have engaged in a flow activity and experienced a flow state, reflect on your experience. Ask yourself the following questions:

  a. Did you lose track of time?

  b. Did you forego breaks?

  c. Did you want to do it?

  d. Did you feel immersed in the task?

  e. Were you challenged but not overwhelmed?

6. Make a note in your journal or calendar about how you feel afterward. Share your reflection on experiencing flow with someone else. (Savor it!)

PERMA Exercise

As Seligman contends in the PERMA theory, five areas contribute to overall life satisfaction and well-being. It is important to first identify specific behaviors we exhibit that exemplify each of the five factors. Then, as in the flow exercise, we try to cultivate opportunities to incorporate existing or new behaviors for each PERMA area into our lives with regularity. This exercise will help you examine your current behaviors in each area and how you might increase the quantity or frequency to further enable well-being.

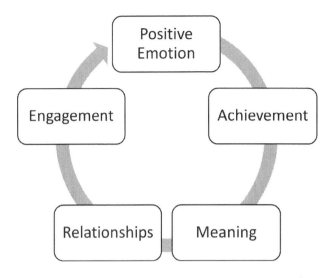

Figure 13.3: Examining the PERMA wheel

1. Seligman's PERMA theory identifies the five elements required to flourish. For each element, write down any behaviors or activities you currently do that support each element in the pie chart. Try to think of as many examples as you can for each. For example:

Relationships

- I spend time daily with my children, playing, talking with them, and helping them with homework.

- I eat lunch with coworkers every day.

- I call my family members every Sunday.

Meaning

- I volunteer at my church as a visitor to sick members of the congregation.

- I am trying to raise healthy and kind children.

Positive emotion

- I listen to my favorite music during my commute.

- I read a novel for pleasure for a half hour every night.

- I share funny videos with my friends on social media.

2. When you are finished, look at the wheel and notice if there is any balance or imbalance among the five areas. Were some areas easier to identify examples? Are some areas blank? For those areas where few behaviors are listed, think about what you could do to expand in that area. Jot these down in the margins outside the pie chart.

3. Set a time frame in which you will begin to incorporate these new behaviors into your life. For example, perhaps you decide you would like to reconnect with an old friend who has been out of touch. You could write "Call Sandra—within the next month," and then actually put it into your calendar when you can make time for it. But according to PERMA, continuous behaviors matter more than occasional occurrences. So if you do decide to reconnect, make it a regular frequency, like call once a month or invite Sandra into your social media connections. Singular occurrences are insufficient.

CHAPTER 14
Tipping the Positivity Scale

While PERMA introduced positive emotion as a component in flourishing, Barbara Fredrickson went on to *quantify* just how much is needed and to what degree positivity versus negativity impacts our ability to see significant benefit. Fredrickson also defined positive emotion more fully and studied specific aspects for their impact on physiological and psychological health.[31]

Her positivity theory recognizes the importance of factors such as love and other positive emotions in well-being. Again, relatedness and connection to others is critical to this theory of wellness. There are many similarities to Seligman's PERMA theory and Ryan and Deci's basic psychological needs. The converging of theories and consistency of their findings contributes to our growing body of wellness knowledge and evidence-based practices.

Fredrickson developed the broaden-and-build theory, which holds that experiencing positive emotion creates additional resources within us that we can draw from and essentially build our reserves.[32] These reserves help buffer periods of hardship and create resilience.

The Positive Emotions

Fredrickson studied the physiological effects of positive emotion.

She demonstrated how we have the ability to take control over our experiences and uncovered the effects in the body when we change our behavior and thoughts. Her study of the interrelationship of mind and body, specifically how our thoughts and behaviors affect the body, is groundbreaking and came to the forefront of positive psychology.

So, what do we mean exactly by positive emotion or positivity? Fredrickson identified and studied ten of the most common positive emotions. Some are obvious, others may surprise you. These are the ten positive emotions Fredrickson studied:

☺ joy

☺ gratitude

☺ serenity

☺ interest

☺ hope

☺ pride

☺ amusement

☺ inspiration

☺ awe

☺ love

Fredrickson describes *joy* as an unexpected good fortune, receiving good news, a pleasant surprise. Joy creates the urge to play and get involved. As a byproduct of joy, we acquire skills through experiential learning prompted by the joy.

In *gratitude*, we acknowledge another person as the source of unexpected good fortune. It creates the urge to creatively consider new ways to be kind, and a byproduct of gratitude is generosity.

Fredrickson describes *serenity* as contentment, when we have the feeling that current circumstances are just right or satisfying or should be cherished. This is when we are feeling comfortable and at ease. Often with serenity we have the urge to savor, and these feelings contribute to the formation of new priorities or values. We can better define the self.

Interest is the emotion we experience when feeling alert or curious. It happens when we experience something novel, mysterious, or challenging, yet not overwhelming. It creates the urge to explore and expand the self. From interest we develop skills or knowledge.

Hope is an inherently uplifting emotion. Often hope occurs in grim situations, but it also enables people to envision a chance that things might change for the better. Hope creates the urge to garner one's own resources to turn things around, foments optimism, and fosters resilience.

Pride occurs when we feel confident or self-assured, having attained a socially valued achievement or met a goal. Experiencing pride is validating to the self.

Amusement is feeling silly and often involves laughter. It occurs in not serious social situations and results in strengthening social bonds.

Inspiration is the witnessing of human excellence that uplifts us, regardless of our abilities. We can appreciate the talents and achievements of others. Inspiration motivates us for personal growth.

Awe is felt when we encounter beauty or goodness on a grand scale, feeling overwhelmed with wonder. Awe changes our views of the world.

Love encompasses all the positive emotions felt in an interpersonal relationship. Love is a feeling of mutual caring, closeness, and trust. It can include romantic love, familial love, friendships, and more.

The research found that any of these ten emotions imparts the same psychological boost. While we can easily understand love and joy as a source of positive emotion, they are perhaps more elusive. The others, however, are more accessible sources of positive emotion and can be more easily cultivated in our lives. For example, it is free and simple to experience gratitude, and the practice of gratitude has been incorporated into many wellness initiatives as a means of battling depression. Keeping a gratitude journal and writing heartfelt thank-you notes help us and those we thank, becoming a source of positivity experienced and bestowed.

We can fairly easily increase our interest by engaging in hobbies, clubs, and other activities to expand on our skills and abilities. Many coaching clients find interest to be one of the easiest positive emotions to access, and in the coaching process they often rediscover joy in pursuing long-abandoned hobbies. As easy as going to a public library or searching online, information is so readily available for virtually any area of interest. It becomes a matter of devoting some time on a regular, frequent basis for pursuing your interests.

There are some positive emotions that not only benefit us but also become a source of positivity for others. Like gratitude, amusement and hope affect others as much as they help to elicit positive emotion in ourselves. Sharing a joke with a coworker, offering hope to someone undergoing hardship, and expressing thanks to those whose actions impacted us are simple behaviors that pack a power-ful push of positivity. When we try to quantify our experiences of positive emotion, amusement is an area in which we can easily boost our numbers with little thought and effort.

Why would we want to quantify our experience of positive emotion? Fredrickson went on to quantify the amount of positivity needed to attain a tipping point of transformation. She developed the Losada ratio of three-to-one ratio of positivity to negativity and describes the building of positive emotion as an upward spiral of thought and actions. Let's look more directly at her findings.

Working with Chilean organizational psychologist Marcial Losada, Fredrickson developed a mathematical model and deter-mined that the ratio above which we flourish is three-to-one, below which we languish. That means we need to experience positive emotion three times as much compared to negative emotion in order to gain benefits from positivity. It is the tipping point for whether we languish or flourish. The positive emotions, unfortunately, tend to be more fleeting, and negative emotion tends to remain with us longer; they are said to be stickier. Recall the negativity bias from chapters 3 and 12—our brain dwells on negative thoughts, threats, and experiences. To counteract that negativity bias, the frequency of positive emotion must increase. Positive emotion is crucial to our well-being. The lighter positive emotions can counterbalance the heavier negative emotions. So to promote optimal functioning, happiness, or flourishing, we must deliberately cultivate and create opportunities for positive emotion. We don't need to brainstorm about negativity—there's plenty of that around without trying.

What Does Positive Emotion Do for Us?

While positive emotion sounds good, it is more than just a warm and fuzzy, feel-good experience. We see measurable physiological effects. It is certainly not only a mind game. The brain and body are inextricably linked as demonstrated by researchers worldwide replicating outcomes in boardrooms, laboratories, classrooms, social communities, and diverse populations. When we feel good, our body language shows it. We have a spring in our step, our posture is erect and slightly forward, we subjectively and objectively feel better. But if that's still not enough to convince naysayers about the power of positivity, how might they feel about a reduced mortality rate? Positive emotion experiences have been associated with greater longevity! Would naysayers be interested if we created a success generator? Positivity generates success as much as it is a byproduct of success. Are we successful because we flourish, or are we flourishing because of our success? Behaviors of flourishing breed success, but success is not necessary for flourishing. Indeed, there are countless news stories of people in intolerable circumstances who are somehow able to rise above and feel content, even happy.

Still there are many who disparage positivity. Yet when we consider the alternative, there seems to be no contest. Positivity transforms our future. Those emotions accrue and build our reserves, which will sustain us in times of despair. Like our weekly bank deposits to a savings account, our positivity practices add up and yield compound interest. Accrued positivity (over weeks or months) builds our internal resources. We sleep better and are more physically healthy. Positivity squashes negativity: the brain cannot experience both at once. We see a physical reduction in blood pressure and heart rate. We see changes in hormonal levels. We become more mindful of situations and more optimistic. We bounce back more easily, and perhaps more quickly, from setbacks. We connect better with others socially, at work, and with customers and colleagues, which increases our sense of well-being. And positivity does not have to be a high-magnitude event like winning the lottery, receiving a Nobel Prize, or getting engaged. It can be mild in magnitude. Fredrickson showed that mild and frequent experience of positive emotion is enough to reap its benefits.

In coaching for positivity, establishing a goal of *mild and frequent* positivity is sustainable and sufficient for effective transformation. Many clients get discouraged, aiming for a big (and vague) goal of being "happy." By refocusing their efforts to mild and frequent experience of positive emotion, those small wins build and accrue to create a noticeable difference. As Fredrickson states in her broaden-and-build theory, positivity broadens our awareness—our minds open and close with the presence and absence of positivity. Our brains start to promote more global thinking. After experiencing positive emotion, we take in more details, recall more information, consider more possibilities, generate more options, are more creative, and are better problem-solvers. Any thinking organization would benefit from fostering these superlatives among their employees.

While good feelings are fleeting, over time positivity has lasting effects. Positivity is nonlinear—it grows geometrically. Rather than a sloped line, the effects of positivity are more aptly displayed as an exponential growth curve. Imagine an upward spiral—an upward and outward motion or a mushrooming effect. Small changes in behaviors make a big difference. Losada and Fredrickson found the tipping point where transformation occurs, the three-to-one Losada ratio.

In the workplace, this concept has huge implications. When we consider there are things that we can do to help leaders and teams think more globally, come up with more options, and creatively solve problems, any organization can become more high functioning. We can jump-start corporate growth with these practices. Aside from the workplace, life and relationships can improve with better problem-solving, creativity, openness, and awareness too. These assets can immensely impact and transform, moving our lives from ho-hum to better, even fabulous.

A better outlook means better job performance. If employers improve the outlook of their employees, it affects their bottom line in a positive way. In relationships, individuals and couples who dedicate time and deliberately cultivate flourishing behaviors are better able to sustain normal ups and downs. Getting back to that idea of optimal human functioning, who wouldn't want to have a better memory, be more creative, come up with more options, and feel more content?

In summary, here are the physical and behavioral impacts of positive emotion:

✓ improved cardiac vagal tone (heart rate)

✓ lowers blood pressure

✓ increases oxytocin levels

✓ promotes big-picture thinking

✓ brain takes in more information

✓ better memory

✓ consider more possibilities

✓ more creativity

✓ better able to handle stress

The Role of Negativity

Negativity is programmed in our brain. And yet negativity plays a huge role in positivity. Why? Because it is important to acknowledge our hardships, challenges, bad luck, or problems. Then, however, it is crucial to allow ourselves the opportunity to pivot, draw on our reserves, and use the positive emotions to help uplift us. Acknowledge the bad, put some closure on it so it doesn't fester, then pivot to a new stream of thoughts and action. This is a common technique used in CBT (cognitive behavioral therapy) and DBT (dialectical behavioral therapy) clinical practices. Some use the mantra "Drop it—don't dwell!" as a reminder to move on after acknowledging negativity. Positive psychologists are not naïve, believing that bad things do not happen. On the contrary, bad things will happen. Our response to them, however, is within our own control. We can't experience positivity if we never see negativity. Negativity is adaptive to a degree in that our attention to it reduces threats to our survival. However, our brains are perhaps overattuned to negativity and are more likely to seek out negativity than positivity. But we can change that. We can take steps to notice and acknowledge the negative and choose to pivot toward a more positive view and positive action.

Fleeting but Not Fake

Sincerity of positivity is crucial—fake positivity is useless and does not prove effective in eliciting positive emotion. Pasting a smile on your face is not genuine regard. Note, however, that recent research suggests faking it can to some degree elicits sincere benefits. Social psychologist Amy Cuddy has shown that *faking* confidence can bring the real thing about.[33] But while good times fade and time moves on, positive feelings can be made to linger and accumulate in the mind and body. They accrue much like pennies in the bank. And those interest-bearing positivity instances yield dividends in years to come.

Yet myths about positivity persist. Some insist flourishing, or even contentment, is possible only in the absence of negativity; yet only by experiencing negativity can we truly benefit from and experience positivity. Some consider positivity is all in the mind; yet the brain is an organ within the body. We do see changes in the brain with positive experience, thanks to the functional MRI (fMRI), and we see measurable changes in the body (e.g., heart rate, hormonal levels, respiration, blood pressure). These changes are not insignificant. Detractors also commonly cite life circumstances and situational factors as reasons they don't experience positive emotion. But our very existence as humans encompasses the capacity to experience a full range of emotions. It is even more important in times of hardship to look for and create opportunities for positive emotion to help us cope and recover.

Positivity Path Forward

I hope by now you are convinced that it is critical to be more positive, though it is not a switch we can simply turn on. We can learn and then practice techniques that help us become more positive. How do we do it?

From the converging research findings and consistent evidence, we see themes emerging as outcomes are replicated across cultures and in business, the workplace, interpersonal relationships, laboratory settings, Fortune 500 companies, schools, and myriad other settings of human experience. Behaviors influence our thoughts, and our brain affects behavior as well. We are coming to a paradigm shift—a scientific revolution—concerning wellness. When you think about chemistry and physics, the culmination of thousands of empirical studies and replication is what contributed to fact generation. In psychology, we now see the huge overlap between theories and replicated empirical outcomes in research by Seligman, Fredrickson, Ryan and Deci, Csikszentmihalyi, and many others. We are witnessing a birth of a body of knowledge around psychological well-being. The science is telling us how to become our best selves, be more positive and start flourishing, and improve our physiological well-being through efforts of the mind and behaviors that can be measured, taught, and learned. We know how behavior can influence thought. Once we begin to incorporate these lessons into our parenting, education systems, workforce training, and management, we will begin to foster a resilience and strength among people that they can develop for themselves, permeating every aspect of their lives.

Get Back to Play

Work-life balance is a buzz word that has been around since the 1980s. Balancing work and play, however, is not just a feel-good fad or lexicon of the decade. Americans characteristically harbor the need to achieve. A strong work ethic and capitalism contribute to our concept of work-life balance. Americans are busy working, with little time left to devote elsewhere. I like to joke, "Busy is the new black." It has become fashionable to be busy! Yet we're so busy we often fail to notice the goodness in the world.

If we start growing our play ethic (plan mini vacations throughout your day, practice meditation, manage stress, glean opportunities for positivity) we become more like that inner toddler. We open our heart and mind to goodness. Do something enjoyable and fun on a regular basis. This could mean forcing ourselves to take breaks, avoiding working through lunch, planning how to get some outside time or exercise into the workday, or holding meetings with a colleague while walking around the building or downtown along the river. We can choose to drive the scenic route to and from work occasionally. As a leader, boss, or business owner, we can model these behaviors for our employees, and they too may be inspired to incorporate self-care into their workday and reap the benefits. We must *actively practice* those behaviors that meet the three basic psychological needs, satisfy the PERMA elements and those that elicit a flow state, and cultivate opportunities for positive emotion.

Build Yourself

Make *you* a priority. Choose sources of positivity that build you. Examine any faulty logic you may harbor; for example, "If I work more, I will make more money, I will please my boss," and so on. Does this kind of thinking build you? Probably not. A healthier alternative exists; for example, "If I spend that extra hour with my family/to get some exercise/on my hobby/on activities that *build* me, I am ultimately a happier, more productive, and engaged employee/boss/leader." Ask yourself, "What is it that *builds me*?" Reexamine the sources of positivity in your life. Keep a journal and record all instances of positive and negative emotions you experience throughout the day. Work to increase the sheer number of times you felt positive emotion. Focus on increasing how often you experience the lighter positive emotions. Find ways to build your positivity ratio (aim for three to one or higher). Once you identify this, you can purposefully build that into your routine. In doing so, you build your reserves and create your own tool kit from which to draw in challenging times—and start seeing benefits.

Mild and Frequent

Think of the weekend athlete. Aside from its physical risks, exercising every five or six days does not meet the mild and frequent criteria. It is typically more intense and less frequent than a daily regimen. In stark contrast, a clear way to flourishing is to build more positivity into every day. Each of these moments builds up, positivity is additive, and with it our lives grow and flourish! Even if you work long hours, consider how you can make your work more enjoyable: can you walk to meetings, meet in person with others instead of via conference calls, talk more with colleagues, personalize your workspace, savor accomplishments, wear headphones and listen to music, or perhaps alter the ergonomics of your office? There are all kinds of ways to bring more enjoyment into our day. A bit of creativity and outside-the-box thinking is called for. Magnitude is not required, but frequency does matter.

Gary, an accountant for a large tax preparation firm, found himself dreading the upcoming tax season. Throughout the fall months, Gary was increasingly anxious and contemplated quitting his job. He considered how he might make it through what was sure to be a busy, stressful first quarter due to the long days and weekend work required during tax season, based on his experience the prior six years. Gary started keeping a journal of emotion. Not particularly interested in writing a journal, Gary used a simple Excel spreadsheet that he filled in for each day to record any experiences of the ten positive emotions. A second chart held a line for negative emotions. For each day, Gary recorded a few words to capture emotions. Below is an initial entry:

Date	Monday 1/11/20	
Positive Emotion	**Source**	**Negative Emotion**
Joy		Stressed—worked thru lunch
Awe	Saw blue jay in the backyard feeder	Frustration—boss added another client to my assignments
Amusement	Watched You-Tube video of package pirates opening glitter bomb	Disappointment—friend canceled Saturday plans
Love	Sister called to catch up	
Hope		
Gratitude		
Inspiration		
Serenity		
Interest	Played the guitar 35 minutes	
Pride		
Ratio +/-	4	3

The chart also helped Gary quantify the amounts of emotion he experienced. The sample above showed that although Gary did have some positive notes for the day, there were nearly as many negative items. Tracking over the course of a week, Gary found he was not really getting close to the three-to-one ratio required to see benefit of positive emotion. So we discussed how he could incorporate more of the ten positive emotions into a given day. Gary determined he could easily call friends and family, especially if he used his commuting time to do so, and found he got one more positive emotion (love) each day from the calls. He planned on a scenic drive home one day a week (awe). He started trying to get two guitar sessions in each day, even if it meant breaking the same amount of total time it into two separate practices (interest). He brought a framed photo of himself completing a half-marathon into work (pride) and looked at it often to restore a sense of pride. He scheduled on his calendar time at the end of each day to write a brief email to his assistant or team members to thank them for their hard work (gratitude). In reviewing his journal's early entries, Gary found he was not doing enough to cultivate positivity in his life. Conscious and deliberate effort allowed Gary to devise new ways to add opportunities for positivity into his days, and after just three weeks Gary's journal showed noticeable increase in the positivity ratio. Gary started feeling better about work and noticed he was managing the tax season better this year than last. The exercise served to help Gary discover for himself how he could be an agent in cultivating his own positive emotion.

Make Positivity a Strategy

Though as a coach I work with clients on attaining goals, the process and approach to goals is just as critical. If we make positivity a strategy and think of it not so much as a goal in itself, we introduce an element of sustainability and ongoing practice. My clients who begin to think in this way often realize benefits beyond those they had originally hoped to gain from coaching. In creating a positivity strategy for themselves, they progress not only in a path to greater satisfaction, it also eases the way to whatever goals they had set for themselves. Positivity should not end. There is no end state. Rather, it is an ongoing behavior, as are other life-sustaining behaviors such as eating or sleeping. Investment in the self pays dividends. Develop your interests, resume or establish new hobbies, and acquire new skills.

In today's world we use all kinds of strategies to meet goals: weight loss, fitness, financial (one bank uses a slogan "For the achiever in you"). Why not develop our well-being strategy? That is what it takes—an ongoing practice and strategy to incorporate more of the ten positive emotions into everyday life. We must devise ways to do this. Our brains are preprogrammed to attend to negativity, and it was historically adaptive in an evolutionary sense. We had to be on the alert for threats to our survival. But nowadays, we don't have to worry about encountering wild animals on our way to work or while cooking a meal with friends. We can choose to attend less to negativity and threats and direct our focus elsewhere.

A New Mindset

An outdated way of thinking is that self-care is indulgent. People feel guilty about taking time for themselves. I once knew a woman who regularly booked massages and never disclosed this to her husband. I grew up in a large Italian Catholic family. We know about guilt! Guilt was accepted, and self-sacrifice was considered a virtue; martyrs and saints are worshipped. But now we have a growing body of scientific evidence showing that self-care has profound physical and psychological benefits. Guilt is destructive, maladaptive, and harmful to our health, productivity, and mental status. It is not self-indulgent to strive for optimal human functioning, to be our best selves. The research has enabled a new way of thinking—the idea that we can cultivate, protect, and cherish opportunities that open our hearts and minds—and help ourselves to grow and flourish as adults. Doing an activity because we find it interesting and enjoyable is not only okay, it is crucial to getting on a path toward flourishing, happiness, and optimal experience. And we know these practices improve our physical and mental health. We can measure the physiological effects. This natural and ordinary means of producing good feelings is readily accessible. Direct application of these findings could benefit families, employers, and school systems.

Some groups have been found to do better than others at cultivating and sustaining positivity. Those who meditate and adults over age seventy (one of the more positive aspect of aging) are particularly better at learning and practicing positivity on a regular basis. But all of us can become more self-aware, learn techniques to flourish, increase our sources of positive emotion, and strive to meet our basic psychological needs. Then we, too, can harvest benefits that propel us to a better, more satisfying, and more productive life.

Increase Sources of Positive Emotion

As shown by the three-to-one Losada ratio, if we aim to bring in more positivity than negativity over a period of days or weeks, it makes a difference. (Realistically every day may not yield that ideal ratio). Without negativity, we cannot experience positivity. It is the ratio that matters. To improve your ratio, it helps to first track your experiences of positive and negative emotion in a journal. Over time, you can quantify just how much of each you feel on a daily or weekly basis and measure any improvement in the ratio as you begin to deploy and actively build positivity through the principles of flourishing. Go for the small boosts on a more frequent basis. These accumulate and help build our reserves. The small wins prime our pump. In times of stress, we need to consider doing even more of our positivity practices. Think of it as an upward spiral that builds on itself to expand opportunities and outlook. As Benjamin Zander would say, imagine the possibilities, and notice the upward spiral of change.

Communicate

By means of connected communications, adults can typically satisfy the needs for both self-expression and relatedness through their personal interactions with others. Simply put, we find it satisfying! It becomes an intrinsic motivator. We can use language as a tool in building positivity. Practice positive communications by telling a joke or story, greeting a stranger, reaching out to someone who is down, or expressing gratitude. At home or work there are plenty of opportunities to acknowledge or compliment others' efforts. Use language to reframe a negative experience in a more positive way. These techniques work. They are accessible but not always easy. It takes commitment to dig deep inside yourself to devise ways to elicit enjoyment and to sustain the practices over time, internalizing the flourishing behaviors. You will find it so worth any effort put in. With a better understanding of the research, it is easy to see why it is so important for our brain and body to practice behaviors that promote resilience and enable flourishing. When we learn and practice these behaviors, we can develop our own sustainable strategies to do so. I encourage you to practice these techniques to bring more positivity into your life and start flourishing.

So, what will *you* do to flourish?

Losada Ratio Positivity Exercise

Fredrickson and Losada have determined that we flourish when above a three-to-one ratio of positivity to negativity, below which we languish. That means we need to experience positive emotion three times as much as negative emotion in order to see physiological and psychological change. To improve your positivity ratio, take the following steps:

1. Generate some ideas of various activities that would elicit positive emotion in you and perhaps others. These should be things that can be done in fifteen- to thirty-minute blocks of time or even shorter. Create a list of things you've enjoyed in the past, ways to have fun, relax, be creative, learn something new, contribute to the community, or get involved in things that interest you. Maybe they're simple and quick activities, indoor or outdoor, happen alone or with others.

   Consider the ten positive emotions in Barbara Fredrickson's broaden-and-build theory of positivity. Remember, the theory emphasizes mild and frequent experiences that do not require a large, dedicated amount of time. As in the Flow and PERMA exercises, identify examples of activities that currently help you produce any of the ten positive emotions. It may be useful to first list the ten emotions and come up with activities for each. They can be done either at home or incorporated into your workday.

2. Then try to generate new ways you could bring more opportunities to experience them into your life, thereby building your tool kit and resources to draw from. Baylor University psychologist Michael B. Frisch identified over two hundred activities. In a ten-minute brainstorming exercise, one of my corporate workshop clients generated over 140 ideas. Can you beat that? Below are a few ideas to get you started:

- play my "pick-me-up" playlist of songs

- go for a walk on the beach

- go for a run

- watch cat videos

- work on my car

- plan an outing for the weekend

- play a board game with my kids

- call on an elderly or sick relative

- plan my next vacation

- plant bulbs or garden

- visit joke-of-the-day website

- listen to a podcast

- walk the dog

- clean out a closet or drawer

- send a thank-you email to a colleague

3. Once you have your sources of positive emotion list, post this in your office or kitchen—anywhere you will see it regularly—to remind you what can be done for a pick-me-up. Add to the list as you get new ideas.

4. Think about your upcoming week and set aside time each day to do something from your list. Put some of these periodically in your calendar. It need only be a few minutes for some of them. Go for mild and frequent.

Over time, you can begin to incorporate these readily into your week, building positivity and cultivating simple joys in your life.

AFTERWORD

There is an abundance of information available to us in today's content rich and accessible world. Any aspiring graduate or employee has resources for all kinds of training, knowledge, and references on their journey to a better, more successful, and satisfying life and life's work. Some skills, however, are built from within, and through development in these areas, we grow and construct the fundamental foundation for leading ourselves and becoming a better leader for others. In *Skills That Build,* I hope to have provided insight for readers to coach themselves in crucial areas of personal development that will also carry them far in their professional journey, building success from within while fostering well-being. I hope to have inspired readers to choose their behaviors intentionally and cultivate their skills to enable them to be the best they can be and live up to their full potential. Speaking, listening with empathy, focusing on values and priorities, and thriving through flourishing behaviors become the foundation for all other learning, future success, and fulfillment. After all, these skills *build* us.

NOTES

[1] Koch Entertainment, "Abbott & Costello Who's on First," posted by Rosario Maynard on December 2, 2017, YouTube, https://www.youtube.com/watch?v=Rz3mVAPX_fM.

[2] "Who's on First? By Abbott and Costello," Baseball Almanac, https://www.baseball-almanac.com/humor4.shtml.

[3] Edward L. Deci and Richard M. Ryan, "The 'What' and 'Why' of Goal Pursuits: Human Needs and the Self-Determination of Behavior," *Psychological Inquiry* 11, no. 4 (2000): 227–68.

[4] Richard M. Ryan and Edward L. Deci, *Self-Determination Theory: Basic Psychological Needs in Motivation, Development, and Wellness* (New York: Guilford Press, 2017), 239–561.

[5] Barbara L. Fredrickson, *Positivity: Top-Notch Research Reveals the 3 to 1 Ratio That Will Change Your Life* (New York: Three Rivers Press, 2009).

[6] Rosamund Stone Zander and Benjamin Zander, *The Art of Possibility: Transforming Personal and Professional Life* (New York: Penguin Group, 2002), 27–33.

[7] A fabulous book summarizing a lifetime of work on cognitive bias and behavioral economics is Daniel Kahneman's *Thinking, Fast and Slow* (New York: Farrar, Straus and Giroux, 2011). Required reading for anyone who considers themselves a rational thinker!

[8] Cathy Liska, Center for Coaching Certification, Communication webinar, 2009.

[9] Susan T. Fiske and Shelley E. Taylor, *Social Cognition* (Boston: Addison-Wesley

1984), 161–66.

[10] Fiske and Taylor, *Social Cognition,* 414.

[11] Liska, Communication webinar.

[12] Suzanne H. Lease, "Assertive Behavior: A Double-Edged Sword for Women at Work?" *Clinical Psychology* 25, no. 1 (March 2018).

[13] Tessa M. Pfafman and Bree McEwan, "Polite Women at Work: Negotiating Professional Identity through Strategic Assertiveness," *Women's Studies in Communication* 37, no. 2 (May 2014): 202–19.

[14] Sheryl Sandberg, *Lean In: Women, Work and the Will to Lead* (New York: Knopf, 2013), 19.

[15] Amy Cuddy, *Presence: Bringing Your Boldest Self to Your Biggest Challenges* (New York: Little Brown and Company, 2015).

[16] Cuddy, *Presence.*

[17] Sandberg, *Lean In,* 33–38.

[18] Barbara L. Fredrickson and Daniel Kahneman, "Duration Neglect in Retrospective Evaluations of Affective Episodes," *Journal of Personality and Social Psychology* 65, no. 1 (1993): 45–55.

[19] Michael I. Posner et. al, "Developing Attention: Behavioral and Brain Mechanisms," *Advances in Neuroscience* 2014 (May 2014), https://doi.org/10.1155/2014/405094.

[20] The 50-10-40-percent formula was popularized in work done by positive psychologist Sonja Lyubomirsky, author of *The How of Happiness* (New York: Penguin, 2007). Based on a body of research in this field and utilizing primarily identical twin studies, she and her colleagues argued that approximately 50 percent of variance in happiness is determined by genes, and 10 percent of variance in happiness is determined by life circumstances, leaving the remaining 40 percent within our influence.

[21] "Singin' in the Rain," *Singin' in the Rain,* directed by Gene Kelly and Stanley

Donen, 1952.

[22] Dan Ariely, *Predictably Irrational: The Hidden Forces That Shape Our Decisions* (New York: HarperCollins, 2010).

[23] Daniel Goleman, *Emotional Intelligence: Why It Can Matter More Than IQ* (New York: Bantam, 1995); and Mihaly Csikszentmihalyi, *Flow: The Psychology of Optimal Experience* (New York: Harper & Row, 1990).

[24] Deborah D. Danner, David. A. Snowden, and Wallace Friesen, "Positive Emotions in Early Life and Longevity: Findings from the Nun Study," *Journal of Personality and Social Psychology* 80, no. 5 (2001): 804–13.

[25] Kahneman, *Thinking.*

[26] Colin F. Camerer, "Artificial Intelligence and Behavioral Economics," in *The Economics of Artificial Intelligence: An Agenda,* ed. Ajay Agrawal, Joshua Gans, and Avi Goldfarb (Chicago: University of Chicago Press, 2019), 587–608.

[27] Jacqueline Nesi and Mitchell J. Prinstein, "Using Social Media for Social Comparison and Feedback-Seeking: Gender and Popularity Moderate Associations with Depressive Symptoms," *Journal of Abnormal Child Psychology* 43, no. 8 (2015): 1427–38.

[28] Csikszentmihalyi, *Flow.*

[29] Martin E. P. Seligman, *Flourish: A Visionary New Understanding of Happiness and Well-Being* (New York: Free Press, 2011).

[30] Ryan and Deci, *Self-Determination Theory*, 239–561.

[31] Fredrickson, *Positivity.*

[32] Barbara L. Fredrickson, "The Role of Positive Emotions in Positive Psychology: The Broaden-and-Build Theory," *American Psychologist* 56, no. 3 (March 2001): 218–26.

[33] Amy J. C. Cuddy et al., "Preparatory Power Posing Affects Nonverbal Presence and Job Interview Performance," *Journal of Applied Psychology* 100, no. 4 (February 2015): 1286–95.

ABOUT THE AUTHOR

Gina M. Wilson earned her undergraduate degree from the University of Delaware and holds a Master of Science in Cognitive Psychology from Villanova University. Her interest in leadership psychology began while writing her graduate thesis on employee performance and through extensive experience as a management consultant in the tech and healthcare industries. She received coach training through the Center for Coaching Certification and continued study at the Institute of Coaching at McLean Hospital, a Harvard Medical School affiliate. Gina's unique approach to coaching embraces the convergence of psychology, business, and well-being.

Founder of System Strategies Consulting and Coaching, she is an experienced software developer, healthcare strategist, college instructor, and business owner. Her clients include professionals, business leaders, healthcare systems, higher education and government organizations, nonprofits, small business owners, corporate teams, and adults aspiring to grow personally and professionally. She has served as board member for the Mental Health Association in Delaware and continues to promote mental health practices and awareness. Beyond work, she enjoys paddleboarding, doing Zumba, being outside, and spending time with her family in their coastal Delaware home.

Printed in Great Britain
by Amazon

63717922R00154